Praise for *Follow the Call*

Follow the Call is a masterclass in faithfulness to the gospel and obedience to God's call. Rob Millman and Tim LaFleur don't just write about ministry—they live it. This book is both a guide and an encouragement for anyone wrestling with the call to vocational ministry. Packed with biblical insights, practical wisdom, and inspiring testimonies, it's a must-read for emerging leaders and seasoned pastors alike. It's a timely reminder that the harvest is plentiful, and the laborers must be ready. This book equips you to answer the call with clarity, courage, and Christ-like humility."

Shane Pruitt, National Next Gen Director, North American Mission Board, and author of *Calling Out the Called*

Every Christian is commanded by God to make disciples of all nations, but some are called into full-time vocational ministry. Understanding the difference between the two can be difficult to discern. Rob Millman and Tim Lafleur offer a guidebook for anyone navigating a call to ministry. *Follow the Call* guides the reader through testimonies of those called to ministry, offering decades of ministry experience and tools to help determine if one is called to vocational ministry.

Robby Gallaty, Pastor, Long Hollow Church and author, *Growing Up* and *Replicate*

Follow the Call is a valuable resource for help in discerning one's call to ministry and for the church leaders who affirm this calling. Fueled by the urgency to make disciples of Jesus Christ and filled with practical tools for equipping in this holy task, it's a must-read for men in our generation and for those training up the next.

Tony Merida is the founding pastor of Imago Dei Church in Raleigh, N.C, and is the vice president of Planter Development for Send Network. He also serves as a Board member for The Gospel Coalition.

Rob Millman and Tim LaFleur offer biblical guidance and practical advice to help men know whether or not God is calling them into vocational Christian service. They also offer wise counsel and practical help for Pastors, Associational Mission Strategists, and others in ministry to help men as they follow God's call on their lives.

Dr. Ray Gentry, President/CEO, Southern Baptist Conference of Associational Leaders

Follow the Call by Rob Millman and Tim LaFleur is highly practical and powerful work. It is much needed for all hoping to understand God's plan for their life and prepare for it. This unique book also helps pastors and mentors more effectively minister to the called.

Dr. Dave Earley, associate professor of Pastoral Leadership and Evangelism, Liberty University.

The church is desperate for the next generation of men called and prepared for ministry. Everywhere we turn we hear national leaders speaking about "calling out the called," but what does that mean? Rob Millman and Tim LaFleur have developed an intentional process to help us raise up a new generation of leaders. Whether you're personally struggling with whether God is calling you, or you're pastoring a church and looking for the nuts and bolts of how you can identify and develop future leaders, this book is for you. Its scriptural and practical insights will give you the tools you need.

Dr. Leo A Endel, Executive Director, Minnesota-Wisconsin Baptist Convention; Senior Pastor of Emmanuel Baptist Church, Rochester, MN; adjunct professor of doctoral leadership, Midwestern Baptist Theological Seminary.

Inspiring, Practical, and Essential

Follow the Call is a timely and much-needed resource that reinforces the clear biblical mandate to raise up men who will lead the advancement of God's kingdom through the local church. Rob and Tim provide a biblically grounded, intensely practical, and deeply inspiring guide for pastors and associations seeking to identify, equip, and empower those called to gospel ministry. With sound biblical exposition, seasoned wisdom, and relevant practical counsel, they offer a roadmap for collaborative leadership development.

This book is an invaluable tool for pastors and ministry leaders, equipping them to approach leadership development with clarity, confidence, and a renewed sense of purpose. I highly recommend it to those committed to strengthening the future of gospel ministry through intentional discipleship and mentorship.

Bob Bickford, Executive Director, Nashville Baptist Association

FOLLOW *the* CALL

For Those Aspiring to Christian Ministry and Pastors Mentoring Emerging Leaders

Rob Millman and Tim LaFleur

Follow the Call:
For Those Aspiring to Christian Ministry and Pastors Mentoring Emerging Leaders

© 2025 Rob Millman and Tim LaFleur
All rights reserved.

ISBN 979-8-218-67314-7

Visionary Voices Press
Nashville, TN

Printed in the United States of America

Scripture quotations are taken from the Christian Standard Bible®, Copyright © 2017 by Holman Bible Publishers. Used by permission. Christian Standard Bible® and CSB® are federally registered trademarks of Holman Bible Publishers.

"How, then, can they call on him they have not believed in? And how can they believe without hearing about him? And how can they hear without a preacher? And how can they preach unless they are sent? As it is written: How beautiful are the feet of those who bring the good news."
—Romans 10:14–15

Dedication

Rob

I am deeply grateful to those who have discipled me—especially my pastors, teachers, parents, and grandparents. Thank you to my brother Mark, Tim LaFleur, and the Follow the Call Advisory Council for joining me in raising up pastors for ministry. Above all, to my wife Lisa—your devotion to our Lord Jesus Christ inspires me. I love you!

Tim

I want to dedicate this book to Conrad and Carmen Bieber who mentored and discipled me as a new believer. Thank you so much for modeling what it means to follow Jesus! To all of the godly men who invested in me through the years. Your patience and love have motivated me to invest in others (2 Timothy 2:2). To my wife Chris, my children, and my grandchildren. I'm so thankful for all of you and the joy and blessing you are to my life.

Also, special thanks to Rob Millman. I am so thankful for your friendship and fellowship in the gospel.

Contents

Foreword 13
Introduction Follow the Call 17
Prologue 19
Prayer Requests 21
Our Call to Ministry Testimonies 23

Section 1: Wrestling with the Call of Ministry 27
Chapter 1: Am I Called? 29
Chapter 2: Where God is at Work 39
Chapter 3: Next Steps While You Wait 49

Section 2: Timothy: His Life and Lessons in Leadership 59
Chapter 4: A Study on One Who Was Called 61

Section 3: Mentoring Emerging Leaders 73
Chapter 5: How to Relate to a Man God Can Shape 75
Chapter 6: Mentoring Emerging Leaders 85
Chapter 7: Make Your Investment Count 93
Chapter 8: Intentionally Calling the Younger Generations 101

Section 4: Ministry Toolbox 105
Chapter 9: Call-to-Ministry Testimonies 107
Chapter 10: Call-to-Ministry Sermons 121

Final Thoughts 147
Appendices 149
About Follow the Call 161
A Final Word 167
About the Authors 169

FOREWORD

Only three years after the commencement of my walk with Christ, I felt a movement of the Holy Spirit, a definite call of God on my life. Though I could not possibly understand all that it meant, I had some insight into its implications. I was, after all, born into a pastor's home. I had witnessed the unrelenting demand of study and sermon preparation, the constant requests to visit and pray with the sick and elderly, and the quiet, sullen nights in the parsonage after a contentious church business meeting.

The greatest obstacle that deterred me, however, was none of those challenges nor a fear of ministry itself. I feared a far more imposing impediment and trembled before a deeper and more daunting difficulty than anything I had seen in my father's duties. I was so intimidated by a single issue that I questioned whether I was fit for the ministry, and whether anyone would believe I was genuinely called by God.

My great problem was that I was only ten years old.

Who would believe a ten-year-old kid was genuinely called by God, set apart to serve the church, and preach the Word? I wasn't sure I did. Yet as conscious of the optics and filled with self-doubt as I was, I had an inner burning compulsion that I could not suppress or ignore. Every time I heard the Word preached, I felt the need to declare publicly that God had called me and I had answered him. Still, I feared what everyone, especially my dad, would say about a young boy claiming that God had called him into ministry.

Finally, one afternoon I could keep silent no longer. I had to unburden myself to my father and gauge his opinion on the matter. A garden lay between the parsonage and the church, and I can still recall as I walked beside it how felt as though my heart would pound out of my chest. Upon entering the church and then his study, I saw him sitting at his desk typing a sermon outline on his IBM Selectric perched on a small side table, Bible open, books fanned across the metal desktop.

I sat silently, waiting for him to stop his work and look up, but when he did, I still said nothing, which he recognized as unusual.

"What's up?" he asked, easily recognized that something was troubling me.

"I don't know how to say this," I began. "I know people will say that I am only doing it because you're my dad. I know they'll say that I'm just a kid and don't know what I am talking about. I know it looks *weird* . . . but . . ."

"What?" he asked after waiting patiently and then recognizing I needed prompting. "What is going on?"

"Dad," I said, beginning to choke up and straining to push the words out without air from my lungs, "I think God is calling me to preach."

I was certain his response would go one of two directions. Either he would tell me not to worry about what people thought or else he would tell me to inwardly answer the call but wait a while to be sure. I wasn't sure which he would say, nor which I wanted him to say.

Then he gave me perhaps the best advice I've ever received.

"Hersh," he said, if God calls you when you are ten, you ought to say 'yes' when you are ten. There will be plenty of time for God to confirm his call and refine his call and show you the next steps. But for now, just get in the habit of saying 'yes' to God. Whatever he requires, whatever it costs, as soon as he reveals it to you, just always say 'yes' to God."

It was the best possible advice for a ten-year-old boy struggling with a call he could not possibly comprehend, and it has proved the right advice for every stage of life and every move of God ever since. I settled it in my mind that afternoon that I would simply say 'yes' to God and leave the details up to him to reveal in time and in whatever manner he chose. When I was eighteen and a freshman in college, I revisited that decision and confirmed it once again. I have enjoyed a life of ministry and of fellowship with Christ, as well as decades of training others for ministry and service to the Lord.

That advice my father gave to his bewildered boy has been an invaluable encouragement, my core commitment, and the posture of my heart ever since, but it has also been the counsel I have shared with thousands of others, especially as they have wrestled with whether God was calling them to ministry and to which particular form of service to Christ.

Yet as good as that advice remains, I realize that even people who are committed to saying 'yes' to God whatever he asks of them nonetheless often have trouble understanding what, specifically, he is asking of them. That is why I am so grateful to Rob Millman and Tim LaFleur for providing such a stimulating and clarifying tool for those that might be wrestling with whether or how God is leading them. Steeped in Scripture, filled with helpful examples and proven principles, this is the kind of book that God can use to help an entire generation find their place of ministry.

The journey of discerning God's call to ministry is both profound and deeply personal, but it should not be separated from the godly influence of other faithful believers. It may be filled with introspection, prayer, and even uncertainty, but it also needs to be subjected to sound biblical counsel and the patterns of the way God has moved in the lives of others.

In this tremendously helpful volume, Rob and Tim have offered profound insights yet elegantly simple tools to answer the tough questions and prepare seeking Christians for the divine mission ahead. They share wisdom, biblical insights, and personal anecdotes that illuminate the process of discernment. But they also provide clear suggestions for Christian leaders and mature believers to shepherd others through the process of discerning God's call, determining God's will, and surrendering to God's Spirit. Their practical and insightful approach will help anyone at any age wondering if God might be setting them apart for service.

In a world of distractions and inducements to a self-centered life, hearing and interpreting the voice of God becomes a sacred pursuit. Thankfully, this book is a guide for those who find themselves at the crossroads, yearning to understand whether the King has singled them out for special service in his Kingdom. I am confident that these pages can help everyone who reads it learn what a blessing awaits those who just say "yes" to God.

Hershael W. York
Dean, School of Theology
The Southern Baptist Theological Seminary

Introduction

Follow the Call

This book is about those who feel the call of Jesus to follow him, to love and serve others. As the authors of the book, we have a compelling desire to share Jesus with everyone. We have a true burden for the lost, and our deepest desire is for those who know Jesus to develop and grow into mature disciples who make disciples. This book is written to those who feel a call to ministry to provide a man insights in discernment and provide next steps for those sensitive to understanding God's plan for their life. This book is also written for those engaged in ministry to encourage them to disciple, lead, and develop emerging leaders.

We want to help those called and their pastors to connect the dots by providing a platform and tools to encourage spiritual growth for both those called and those who have accepted the call. Throughout the church age, there has always been an urgent need to raise up men to become leaders, and the same is still true in this moment. This book is written to provide knowledge and practical steps to be useful in advancing the cause of Christ in understanding the concept of calling.

This book is comprised of four sections. The first is dedicated to the man discerning the call to ministry. We want the chapters in this section to provide clear insight to what is involved in wrestling with the call of God upon one's heart. We also provided an overview and examples of where men can be of service, as well as next steps because a call to ministry is a call to prepare. In the very middle of this book—as a transition—we include a study on Timothy and how he honored God with his life. The second portion of this book is dedicated to assisting pastors to lead emerging leaders. This section is based upon Tim LaFleur's forty-plus years of experience in making disciples, raising up leaders, and being an encourager. These chapters reflect upon investing in men and the importance of nurturing and developing relationships to guide emerging leaders in the church.

The idea of this book was birthed out of our deep desire to grow the church by helping men to follow the call of Jesus. As we see it, there are three calls: first, the call to salvation; second, the call to sanctification and service; and third, the call to ministry leadership. The high call to priesthood dates back to the time of Aaron in Exodus 4 when God called upon him to speak to the people. Some may say the call stretches even earlier, to the time of Melchizedek. But this we do know: Jesus is our example of the great high priest. The reason for our faith is the example he provided in his life on earth, his sacrifice he made to pay for our sins, and his resurrection to pronounce victory over death and hell provides us evidence and reason to proclaim Jesus as Lord.

More than ever, we need godly pastors to encourage active discipleship, to be intentional in raising up men to be leaders, and to walk alongside of those who are sensitive to the call of ministry. We also need those men who feel God's calling upon their lives not to shirk back but to actively discern the call, pray for guidance, and reach out to leaders to provide them with next steps and determine if their call is affirmed.

"Then I heard the voice asking: Who will I send? Who will go for us? I said: Here I am send me" (Isa 6:8).

Prologue

The next day, John was standing with two of his disciples. When he saw Jesus passing by, he said, "Look, the Lamb of God!" The two disciples heard him say this and followed Jesus. When Jesus turned and noticed them following him, he asked them, "What are you looking for?" They said to him, "Rabbi" (which means "Teacher"), "where are you staying?" "Come and you'll see," he replied. So they went and saw where he was staying, and they stayed with him that day. It was about four in the afternoon. Andrew, Simon Peter's brother, was one of the two who heard John and followed him. He first found his own brother Simon and told him, "We have found the Messiah" (which is translated "the Christ"), and he brought Simon to Jesus. When Jesus saw him, he said, "You are Simon, son of John. you will be called Cephas" (which is translated "Peter")."

—John 1:35–42

In the first chapter of the Gospel of John, we learn that Andrew was the first disciple to follow Jesus. He shared with his brother that "we have found the Messiah" and encouraged him to listen to Jesus. The very next day Jesus found Philip and told him, "Follow me." Philip shared with Nathaniel about Jesus, and when he met him, Nathaniel believed that Jesus was the Messiah. Later, Jesus called Matthew by simply saying, "Follow me."

> "As Jesus went on from there, he saw a man named Matthew sitting at the tax office, and he said to him, 'Follow me,' and he got up and followed him" (Matt 9:9).

The Scriptures from the Old to New Testament provide many pictures of men and women who followed the call of God upon their hearts. Abraham in the desert conversed with God, and the words "here I am" are echoed by Jacob, who responded to a vision, Moses at the burning bush, and Anaias's response before meeting Saul in Damascus. Isaiah likewise responded to the Lord by saying, "Here I am, send me" (Isa 6:9).

What about you, how will you respond?

Prayer Requests

"In every generation the church needs a new corps of preachers and leaders, ministers and missionaries. Our Lord taught us to pray for workers for the harvest, and so we must."
–R. Albert Mohler, Jr.

Dear Heavenly Father,

We ask for you to make an impression upon the hearts of men in all four corners of this world who have been impacted by the gospel message and are truly called to herald your Word to the masses. We pray for the Holy Spirit to raise up men in the ministry to become preachers of your word, pastors to shepherd your people, and missionaries to reach everywhere. Lord, we lean upon your strength to touch the hearts of those you have called to pursue the ministry and reveal your plan to each and every man. We are grateful for your presence in our lives and for those who have faithfully preached the gospel message and taught us your Word. We ask for your hand upon this ministry to be a spark and a catalyst in every church we reach to disciple pastors and raise up men to follow your call to fulfill the Great Commission and make your Word known. In Jesus's most holy and precious name we pray, Amen.

Prayer is one of the greatest gifts God has given us to communicate with him. Here are some of our requests we ask for you for you to pray.

Requests for Individuals

Pray for God to impact the hearts of men to follow the call into ministry.

Pray for men who have been called to fully surrender to Christ.

Pray for men to seek the Lord upon considering a call, to pray, read, learn, and seek counsel.

Pray for mission opportunities for those discerning a call to check their heart and serve others.

Requests for Pastors

Pray for pastors to call upon men in messages, public events, and privately to consider the call.

Pray for pastors to disciple and shepherd with love those who are discerning a call to ministry.

Pray for pastors to implement residency building processes in their church to raise up workers.

Requests for Local Churches

Pray for church leaders to be supportive to assist men considering a call to ministry.

Pray for the church to be a place where seeds for ministry may be planted, grow, and thrive.

Pray for churches to be mission minded to help men grow.

Requests for the Greater Church

Pray for church associations to proactively raise up and support men to consider ministry.

Pray for church associations to provide learning opportunities

Pray for the church to work together to proactively be on mission locally and globally!

Our Call to Ministry Testimonies

Tim LaFleur's Call to Ministry Testimony

"Therefore, if anyone is in Christ, he is a new creation. The old has passed away; behold, the new has come" (2 Cor 5:17).

In the summer of 1972, as an older teenager, I came to know Christ as Lord and Savior. God, in his grace, allowed me to go to a student camp where I was able to not only hear the gospel but to see it demonstrated in the lives of the students at the camp. What makes my story so unusual is that this was the first time that I heard the simple message of the gospel.

You see, I grew up in a small town in south Louisiana. Like most in my community, I was brought up Roman Catholic, and although I knew a lot about God, I didn't know Him personally. I had "religion," but I didn't have a relationship with Jesus. In fact, I didn't know one Bible believing Christian in my hometown.

As you can imagine, when I came back home from the week at camp, I didn't know what to do or how to grow in my newfound faith. Thankfully, a student leader gave me a Bible and suggested that I begin reading the New Testament (he had highlighted several passages that I should give special attention to).

As I began to read the Word of God, I had this deep desire to immerse myself in it. In fact, I couldn't get enough of the Bible—spending hours at a time reading and meditating on the Scriptures. The more I read, the more I desired God's Word. I had so many questions.

Someone told me that at the little Baptist church they studied the Bible. So, the next Sunday, I showed up with my Bible in hand, ready to receive all that God had for me. I can only imagine what the student leaders thought the day I showed up at church. I am so grateful that they realized that I had a life-altering experience with the Lord, and they helped me grow and mature in my faith.

Conrad Bieber, our student leader, took the time to invest in me spiritually. He not only taught me Christian concepts, but he also modeled before me what it meant to follow Christ. He did a kind of life-on-life discipleship with me that changed my life. I learned how to pray because he prayed with me. I learned how to share my faith because I watched him do it. I learned how to memorize Scripture because we did it together. I can truly say I wouldn't be the man I am today if Conrad hadn't invested in me during those formative years.

When I graduated from high school, I went to college at Louisiana State University (LSU). During my time there and after doing summer missions in North Carolina, I felt God's call to ministry leadership. During the summer, an older college pastor helped me work through God's call on my life and figure out my next steps.

As I look back over the years of ministry, I am amazed by God's faithfulness! Whether it's been the time I spent on a college campus doing collegiate ministry (twenty years) or pastoring in small, medium-sized, or megachurch roles, I have had a burden to walk alongside pastors, church staff, and emerging leaders to help them discern God's calling on their lives and try to figure out their next steps. It's been my great joy to coach and mentor scores of men and women as they follow Christ and live out their God given calling.

Rob Millman's Call to Ministry Testimony

"The one who pursues righteousness and faithful love will find life, righteousness, and honor" (Prov 21:21).

When I was a young boy in first grade, my pastor J. V. Moyer spoke of being "fishers of men," and the first thing I wanted to be when I grew up was a pastor. I attended parochial school except for my second-grade year. I remember my first opportunity for "show and tell" in the southern Indiana public school where I shared Mark 4:35–41 from the devotional book that my mother would read to my siblings and me about how Jesus calmed the winds and the waves. Moving ahead to my senior year at Purdue University, I felt a longing to attend seminary; however, I dealt with mild dyslexia and did not feel I could pass all the required courses and that I wasn't smart enough. However, my desire to the serve Lord remained, and I told those who truly knew me that I would become a missionary later in life.

My upbringing was in the Lutheran Church Missouri Synod. My great grandparents were one of a few couples who in 1900 started the new congregation in Brownstown, Indiana. My grandfather started the Sunday school and was chairman of the congregation in 1953 when they laid the cornerstone for a new building. As an adult, I was very active in the church, serving as an elder for six years. I then served as a school board member at the school that my congregation, along with two other rural churches, worked together to provide Christian education—as part of our churches' ministries—for 175–180 students attending kindergarten through eighth grade. I also taught an adult Sunday school class and organized the community National Day of Prayer breakfast for ten years. A few years later I was chosen to serve as chairman of the congregation during a time when our church struggled. There were over seven hundred members on our rolls, and I learned much during this period of time when there was division and much healing was required. It was through that experience that I truly embraced Colossians 3:12–14.

Fast forward: I began attending Long Hollow Baptist Church in Hendersonville, Tennessee in 2016. In the summer of 2018, while at a Lifeway men's conference and upon listening to Crawford Loritts and my pastor Robby Gallaty, my aspiration to serve in ministry leadership was rekindled. Early in the Fall I enrolled in an expository preaching class taught by Pastor Robby and Gus Hernadez. I immediately followed that class with spiritual disciplines, taught by Tim LaFleur with Robert Hutchinson assisting. I developed confidence and took New Testament with Mark Liverman. Soon after, I applied to Liberty University to enroll in the Christian ministry master's degree program. Tim and Mike Pennington—the Bledsoe Association director—gave me the opportunity to preach my first sermon on a Easter Sunday to a small country church in Sumner County, Tennessee. While finishing my course work in the Spring of 2022, I prayed many prayers asking for God's guidance for what he wanted me to do in ministry. I explored multiple possibilities; he made it very clear to me that I must help men "follow the call." I shared with Pastor Tim how God was working in my life to start a ministry to help men wrestling with the call to ministry, and Tim asked if he could join me. The answer was a simple and joyous "Yes!" He, along with my brother Mark—who serves as a church planting catalyst for NAMB and association mission strategist for the State of Wisconsin—have assisted me to form Follow the Call Ministries.

You see, my relationship with Jesus was founded when I was a young boy, and I have always sensed God's call on my heart to serve him in ministry leadership. My story is not unlike that of many men who felt called and yet did not follow through until later in life. But God in his grace continued to work in my heart and through his Spirit to affirm my calling. Part of my testimony is to be an encourager of others to follow God's call to be of service to preach the Word. No one knows how much time God gives us, but my intention is in the next thirty years to finish well.

In the introduction of Robert Coleman's book *The Masterplan of Discipleship*, he speaks of a ministry lifestyle. He wrote that the Great Commission is a lifestyle "encompassing the total resources of every child of God. Here the ministry of Christ comes alive in the day-by-day activity of discipling."[1] My hope is to assist pastors to mentor, walk alongside, and disciple men of all ages aspiring to serve the Lord, expand the kingdom of God, and bring new souls to Christ.

---

[1] Robert E. Coleman, *The Master Plan of Discipleship* (Grand Rapids: Revell, 1998), 13.

Section 1
Wrestling with the Call of Ministry

Chapter 1

Am I Called?

Rob Millman

There are many men throughout the ages who have felt the call to ministry and occupied pulpits who truly were men of God and made a difference in this world heralding the gospel message. On the other hand, there have also been many men who occupied pulpits who felt a great compelling to be a minister of the Word, but their effectiveness was dulled because, rather than being called by God, they were called by men and compelled by their own spirit rather than the Holy Spirit.

This thought lays out a heavy burden for a man who feels called to the ministry to truly consider what it means to discern a call and serve the Lord Our God as a preacher of the Word.

Prayer

As one begins to consider wrestling with the call of ministry, the first step is to dedicate time for prayer. It is through prayer and conversing with God about his plan for one's life that a man begins to truly distinguish the internal and external signs that God is calling him for service. It is essential to set emotions aside and listen to the Holy Spirit as he affects one's heart and life to consider the question: "Am I doing this for me, or I am I following the guidance of a Holy God to serve him without consideration to my own needs or selfish ambitions?"

Martyn Lloyd-Jones, one of the greatest preachers of the twentieth century, dedicated his life to ministry and served as pastor of Westminster Chapel in London for three decades. In his book *Preaching and Preachers*, Lloyd-Jones wrote, "I would say that the only man called to preach is the man who cannot do anything else, in the sense that he is not satisfied with anything else. This call to preach is so put upon him that he says, 'I can do nothing else, I must preach.'"[2]

Jones's viewpoint removes a burden from the one hesitant about pursuing a call into ministry. A man must be so compelled to want to serve the Lord that he cannot fathom the pursuit of any other vocation. Isaiah wrote, "His delight shall be in the fear of the Lord" (Isa 11:3 ESV). Although this passage describes the coming Messiah, the first sentence of this verse provides a guide for a man considering a call to ministry: "To fear God is to respond to him in awe, trust, obedience, and worship."[3]

In the *Bible Knowledge Commentary*, John Martin notes how this passage relates directly to the consideration of the call: "The Messiah constantly seeks to do what God the Father wants him to do."[4] Is that not what a man seeking a call to ministry truly desires? If so, discover and cleave to what God the Father wants you to do!

You may be a man called by God to preach with such a great anointing that nobody could doubt or question that you are pursuing your true calling and fulfilling your role in God's kingdom. Perhaps you are in the initial stage of sensing the leaning of the Holy Spirit into you to consider a call to serve the Lord. Whatever your particular situation, your next step should be to boldly approach the throne of God in prayer and ask for his will in your life to determine if the desire you feel belongs to you or to the Father.

A slight word of caution: the affirmation of others, including your church family, does not necessarily mean you are called to ministry. Many brothers and sisters will be excited to encourage and affirm a man who is processing what he believes to be God's call without realizing his true motivation. The pursuit of a call to ministry must only come after thoughtfully and prayerfully considering the call while reading Scripture, recommended books on the calling of God, and meeting regularly with multiple men of God who have permission to listen to and speak into our lives. Our God is great, and service to him in ministry is one of the greatest assignments a man can fulfill; it is worth taking this calling very seriously.

---

[2] Martyn Lloyd-Jones, *Preachers and Preaching* (Grand Rapids: Zondervan, 1972), 105.

[3] John Martin, "Isaiah," in *The Bible Knowledge Commentary: Old Testament*, ed. John F. Walvoord and Roy B. Zuck (Colorado Springs, CO: David C. Cook, 1984), 1056.

[4] Martin, "Isaiah," 1056.

Regardless of who you are or what calling you are considering, fix your eyes on Jesus as you prepare your heart for a life of service to him no matter the vocation to which you are called.

A Journey

One of the very first examples of a man questioning whether he was truly chosen by God was Moses. In Exodus 3 Moses encountered God up close and personal when the angel of the Lord appeared to him in a flame of fire within a bush. You and I will most likely never hear the audible voice of God, but Moses certainly did: "When the Lord saw that he had gone over to look, God called out to him from the bush, 'Moses, Moses!'" (Exod 3:4). Can you imagine that moment? Moses must have felt a variety of emotions hearing the audible voice of the Lord, yet he answered. "Here I am." Our encounter with the Holy Spirit may pale compared to Moses's encounter with God, but they share something crucial: both of them are supernatural, and both of them are genuine.

In his book *Am I Called?* Dave Harvey shares that a call is not theoretical; it is personal. It has been the same throughout the ages from Noah to Abraham, Moses to Joshua, David to Solomon, Elijah to Elisha, and into the New Testament from John the Baptist, all the disciples including the apostle Paul to John the Revelator, and now to men in our modern age. You may not have the impact of Martin Luther, William Tyndale, John Calvin, John Knox, or the likes of Jonathan Edwards, Charles Spurgeon, Billy Sunday, or Billy Graham, but if God is calling you, you must fulfill his purpose at this moment in time, no matter how trivial it may seem. What is trivial to man is significant to God.

Jim Eliot, along with four others, were martyred in 1956 on a mission to Ecuador to reach a people group who did not know Jesus. The impact these men have had—inspiring their own families and countless others to mission work—is incalculable. There are men of God all over our world at this moment who may never have their names printed in history books, but our heavenly Father knows them. A call to ministry is not about personal glamour and prestige but rather is something God uses to fulfill his plan and purpose.

God had a purpose for Moses: to lead the Israelites out of bondage and into the promised land. So, when Moses asked why it had to be him,

God answered, "I will certainly be with you" (Exod 3:12). God said that he would be with Moses, but he is also with every person who loves and trusts him. This is why prayer is so important as one considers his call to ministry: God is with those he has called, and he will provide the answer.

This process of discernment is not going to be an overnight journey. As Harvey has written, "This process is an adventure—one that gets pretty serious and requires desperate prayer."[5] The Gospel writers documenting Jesus's prayer life showed how, at every turn, Jesus demonstrated a genuine love for God in knowing the Father was always with him. As a man discerns God's plan for his life, like Jesus, he must realize God is with him and be reminded of this Scripture: "And if you believe, you will receive whatever you ask for in prayer" (Matt 21:22).

As you walk along the path of discernment in your journey to unearth God's direction for your life, embrace humility and obedience as your essential travel companions. Moses questioned his abilities and asked God to send someone else (Exod 4:10–13). God called Moses even though he knew his deficits and the capacity of his ability. What is central to understanding your capabilities through God's eyes is to realize he does not call the equipped; he equips the called. Paul proclaims this mystery in 1 Corinthians 2:1–5.

Paul's ministry was the demonstration of the Spirit's power in Paul's life, not his own capabilities, and the Spirit's power is also demonstrated in your life. As you process this journey, realize it is God's continual unfolding work in your life that maps out the path. A man should be reminded, whether called to ministry or another vocation, that all his work is to be completed to the glory of God.

Every journey belongs only to the one discerning the call; therefore, it is wise to read the Scriptures, pray, and consult with men who have journeyed a similar path. We also encourage you to read books and articles focusing on the call to ministry. You can find these books highlighted on the reading resources tab at FollowtheCall.org.

---

[5] Dave Harvey, *Am I Called?* (Wheaton, IL: Crossway, 2012), 26.

Finding Direction

I first learned how to use a compass back in my Boy Scouts days. Our scoutmaster pointed out there are four cardinal directions, or main points. We know these directions as north, south, east, and west. He taught us how to identify our location and worked with us to learn how to navigate real-life terrain based on the information we saw on the map.

A few years ago, while hiking during the late spring in the Colorado mountains near Leadville, my cousin Ben and a couple of my friends trekked through snow at depths of four to six feet. We were "post holing," where each step in the snow created a deep hole similar to that of a post hole. This caused us to somehow get off course. We had a map that included elevations and a few markings, so I pulled out my compass and Ben was able to determine which direction we should traverse based upon the combination of the markings on the map and the direction provided by the compass. So how does this relate to a man considering a call to the ministry?

A Christian man's map is the Bible. It is his guide, and if he follows the directions as distinctly defined in the Scriptures, it will lead him to follow Jesus Christ. His compass is always pointing toward Christ no matter where he may be. This compass is the Holy Spirit.

The Holy Spirit working in man's heart provides clear direction. The power of the Holy Spirit has influenced many a man seeking God's will to determine if the purpose of his life is to follow the call and proclaim Jesus to the world as pastor, preacher, and teacher. Paul and Barnabas were two such men, as noted in Acts 13:

As they were worshipping the Lord and fasting, the Holy Spirit said, "Set apart for me Barnabas and Saul for the work to which I have called them." Then after they had fasted, prayed, and laid hands on them, they sent them off. So being sent out by the Holy Spirit, they went down to Seleucia, and from there they sailed to Cyprus. (Acts 13:2–4).

In that same chapter, Luke noted there were several wise men at the church in Antioch, and they were worshiping the Lord through fasting and prayer. It had become apparent to these men that Paul and Barnabas were chosen, "set apart by the Spirit's command," and they laid hands upon them, commissioning them to make their first missionary journey. Notice that Paul and Barnabas did not volunteer for this journey. The Holy Spirit sovereignly called them to become full-time missionaries.

Finding direction as you are discerning the Lord's call on your life comes through the obedience of fasting and prayer, and through the guidance of the company you keep. Heed wise counsel and listen to those praying for you and providing spiritual direction. The Lord will commission you through the Spirit to advance with the Lord's call upon your life. Your encounter with the Holy Spirit may not match Paul's Damascus road experience, but that does not make it any less powerful.

In his book *Discerning Your Call to Ministry*, Jason Allen notes, "A call to preach or teach the Word is the distinguishing mark of a call to ministry." He continues, "This is the biblical pattern God calls—God commissions."[6] If the Holy Spirit's impression on your life is so undeniable that there is nothing you would rather do than herald the Word of God, as Martin Lloyd-Jones suggested, then your answer may be clearly revealed. Magnifying God is about having a heart of worship like those men mentioned in Acts 13:1. They were devout in their intent to seek God's will. They worshiped and prayed intently; they fasted, asking for the Lord's hand upon their efforts to advance the gospel.

As you find your direction in this call on your life, focus on the immediate tasks before you as you magnify the Lord in your work, and either in small or large ways, he will reveal his will. In Acts 9 Jesus revealed his will to Paul in a very dramatic way, and there were men like Ananias and other disciples who poured into Paul. As Luke notes, "Saul was with the disciples in Damascus for some time. Immediately he began proclaiming Jesus in the synagogues: 'He is the Son of God'" (Acts 9:19–20).

As you discern your call, pour yourself into the Scriptures, pray for the guidance of the Holy Spirit, seek wise counsel and surround yourself with godly men, and continue to magnify the Lord in all your work. Put off your old self and put on your new self, and God will change you and mold you into what he desires as his instrument for service.

Absolute Surrender

As a man considers the call to ministry, he should remember that it requires a lifetime mindset and is something to be taken seriously. The definition of unconditional commitment is surprisingly obvious: making

---

[6] Jason K. Allen, *Discerning Your Call to Ministry* (Chicago: Moody, 2016), 22–23.

a pledge of assurance without restrictions. It requires dedicating one's life to the hands of the Lord and being faithful to ministry opportunities. In the book of Daniel we read of three men who placed their lives into the hands of the Lord: Shadrach, Meshach, and Abednego (Dan 3).

Daniel noted in this account that King Nebuchadnezzar had made a gold statue ninety feet high and nine feet wide to be worshiped and sent an order that whoever did not bow and worship this statue would be thrown into a fiery furnace. These three men kept their unconditional commitment to the Lord and refused to worship the idol. For their disobedience to the king, they were indeed thrown into the fire. The Lord rescued them so completely that not one hair on their head nor one stitch of their clothing was singed. Nebuchadnezzar praised God (Dan 3:28) and rewarded the men.

Digging into this account, the three men did not exhibit fear, as they knew God could rescue them from the fire. If he did not, it wouldn't matter anyway, because they would not serve any other gods. The precept of this story is that these men would remain faithful no matter the consequences. There will be obstacles as you pursue your calling, and if called, then as you fulfill your calling there will be all kinds of roadblocks. According to Lifeway Research, "pastors reported that 21 percent of those in their congregations had unrealistic expectations of them, 48 percent indicated the demands of ministry are more than they can handle, and 54 percent found their role as pastors overwhelming."[7] A call to ministry is not a call to Easy Street; rather, it requires steadfast faithfulness.

As one examines their heart and passion for ministry, it requires arriving at a point of final surrender. The three men in Daniel's account were all in; they had surrendered their full hearts to God Almighty. Consider how their dreams, plans, hopes, and desires were relegated to the background when worshiping the Lord became their primary aim. They did not let any obstacle get in the way of choosing to stay faithful to God. In the same way, in considering a call to ministry, a man must relegate his own desires, placing them aside to step forward to serve God as a pastor, preacher, or teacher.

Lifeway's statistics do not paint a pretty picture for ministry. It will require fortitude, hard work, and a fervent desire to fulfill one's role as

---

[7] Lifeway Research, *Pastor Attrition Study*, 2021

the Lord's servant. "As you discern God's will for your life, don't run from your calling!"[8] There are multiple biblical examples of men who shrank back from a call from the Lord.

Think of Jonah, the prophet God called to go preach against the evil in Nineveh. He was filled with fear, and rather than jumping on board with God, he jumped on a ship to flee the Lord's presence. Jonah was off course, sailing away from the Lord's plans, and found himself swallowed up by a fish. Suddenly, he prayed from the belly of the fish and was spit out to do the Lord's bidding. Jonah made his way to Nineveh, where he heralded the Lord's proclamation and the people turned to God. The point of this story for a man considering God's call is to listen, pray, and obey.

Because it requires unconditional commitment, a true call is to discover oneself in the midst of where God plans rather than where man plans. It is to realize there are tough places like Nineveh or Babylon. One must realize that even when called to what appears to be a safe place, that does not guarantee life will be easy, as indicated by the statistics cited above.

Many lost people make their way into the four walls of the church every week. Consider Paul's exhortation to Timothy as he noted there are many unholy people, always learning but never able to come to the truth. In 2 Timothy 3:10–11, Paul imparted there will be struggles, encouraging Timothy to hold to his faith, to strive for patience and endurance, and to love others. Paul related that in all the struggles he encountered, God rescued him from them all.

Finally, Scott Pace and Shane Pruitt wrote in their book *Calling Out the Called*: "But if you resist your call, God won't release you from your call. He desires to use you and is determined to use you! So, by faith and with confidence in his faithfulness, we must come to the point of willing surrender and embrace Isaiah the prophet's response. 'Here I am. Send me.'"[9]

Prayer and Discipleship

As one considers the call to pastor, lead and preach, it so easy to become entrenched in the hidden trap of pursuing everything about God without actually truly pursuing him. Our first goal is to have a relationship with

---

[8] Scott Pace and Shane Pruitt, *Calling Out the Called* (Nashville: B&H Publishing, 2022), 27.

[9] Pace and Pruitt, *Calling out the Called*, 29.

Jesus. A call to ministry is the result of true devotion to earnestly deepen a man's intimacy with Christ; there is nothing that supersedes his longing for a deeper relationship with Jesus. Henry Blackaby said it well: "When you lead a person . . . into a relationship where Christ is Lord, everything else follows. You don't have to convince them they need to spend time in God's Word or prayer or in the fellowship or on mission. That's a spontaneous response to a relationship to the living Lord."[10]

The beginning, middle, and end—not just of your calling but of your life—is all tied to your relationship with Jesus. It is so vitally important to separate the confusion of *playing* Christian with *being* a Christian. You must long for Christ to know you and for you to know Jesus, walk with Jesus, love Jesus, and share Jesus. Forge a true connection leading you to advance all your efforts to proclaim Jesus to the world. It is about chasing Jesus, focusing on the gospel, and clarifying your call. As Dave Harvey explains, "Getting a firm and tightening grip on the gospel clears the mental path to more helpfully ponder your call."[11]

Start by developing a vibrant prayer life. Jesus provided an example of an exemplary prayer life. In fact, the Bible provides evidence he prayed before every event in his life. He prayed at his baptism, before choosing his disciples, before multiplying the bread and fish, for God to raise Lazarus, for those who would believe, while in the garden of Gethsemane, and on the cross. In the same way, a man seeking the guidance for a call of ministry must also pray.

Jesus's message to his disciples on the Sermon on the Mount is to pray in private (Matt 6:5–6). Praying alone is a form of private worship where a man can personally connect with God and in his meditation learn of God's will for his life. It is also during this time that a man can fall on his face before God and in an inconsolable manner asking for God to provide him direction. It was Leonard Ravenhill who said, "God doesn't answer prayer. He answers desperate prayer."[12]

We witness Jesus's example at the garden (Luke 22:42–44) where he

---

[10] See Mark Kelly, "Great Commission Resurgence Must Be Fueled by Relationship," *Baptist Press*, November 18 2023, https://blackaby.org/great-commission-resurgence-must-be-fueled-by-relationship/.

[11] Harvey, *Am I Called?*, 19.

[12] Leonard Ravenhill, "Prayer," http://www.ravenhill.org/prayer.htm, Copyright (C) 1995 by Leonard Ravenhill, Lindale, Texas.

pleaded with the Father. Jesus surrendered himself to God's will. A man must likewise surrender his will and listen, observe, and seek the answer provided through the leaning of the Holy Spirit. This is cultivated through a consistent prayer life. A man seeking God's will must be malleable in spirit, realizing that "surrendering to ministry includes a determination to follow God's call wherever it may lead."[13]

A Personal Prayer

Dear Heavenly Father,
I recommit my life to you today and praise you for the new life I have in Christ Jesus. I confess that I am sinful and unclean, and I repent of my sin and ask for your forgiveness. Just as you raised Christ from the dead by your glory, I too may walk in the newness of life. I am thankful for the transforming work of the Holy Spirit in my life because of the blood of Jesus to make me a new creation. Father, please let your Holy Spirit work more deeply in my heart to draw me closer to Christ that I may experience his love more fully. I pray for your power in my life as your instrument to magnify your glory and majesty to the world. I surrender myself to you and pray for your will in my life so that I may walk worthy of you to be fully pleasing to you bearing fruit in every good work. I pray this day Lord for you to provide me with clear discernment and direction. I lay down my ambitions and surrender myself to you to use me as you desire. Father, please direct me as I acknowledge your will for my life is your best for my life. In Jesus's name I pray, Amen

---

[13] Allen, *Discerning Your Call to Ministry*, 125.

Chapter 2
Where God is at Work
Rob Millman

> *"Now without faith it is impossible to please God, since the one who draws near to him must believe that he exists and that he rewards those who seek him." (Heb 11:6)*

Where and how God calls are similar yet unique for every believer. For those called to ministry leadership, discernment is the recognition of his voice and the understanding that it is truly God's call and God's will.

God's call is more than what you received from listening to a pastor or speaker while experiencing an array of emotions and proclaiming the Lord is calling you to surrender to full-time ministry. Rather, a full understanding of the call goes back to the beginning point when a new believer walked forward with their first step to follow Jesus.

The salvation experience varies in form and fashion from person to person. I remember my experience as a young child when I fully placed my faith in Jesus and fully loved him. I was fortunate, as the household where I grew up revered God. Our family was faithful to attend worship services each week, and I received a daily dose of Jesus as I attended a parochial school. I knew at the age of seven that God was calling me to follow him, and I was encouraged to reach out to others as each week our pastor spoke about being fishers of men.

The call to salvation is the first call. A second call for all believers is the call to sanctification—to grow in holiness and Christlikeness. It is to fully surrender to the Holy Spirit and pray for a powerful work in one's life to draw you closer to Christ and to fully understand all the attributes of God.

It is also a general call to ministry to serve others as part of the body of the church.

The calling of others to ministry was always at the forefront of the apostle Paul's agenda. He frequently likened service to God as understanding all the parts of the body and how they functioned together. We see this in Romans 12, 1 Corinthians 12, and Ephesians 4. Notice what Paul wrote in Romans 12:4–8:

Now we have many parts in one body, and all the parts do not have the same function, in the same way we who are many are one body in Christ and individual members of one another. According to the grace given to us, we have different gifts: if prophecy, use it according to the proportion of one's faith; if service, use it in service; if teaching, in teaching; if exhorting, in exhortation; giving, with generosity; leading, with diligence; showing mercy, with cheerfulness.

The call to ministry leadership is to place your "full yes" on the table and be willing to go where he wants you to go. There is a reason we've devoted an entire book to God's calling. It is amazing the many places where God is at work, and it takes special ministry workers with talents, skills and temperaments to fulfill the work at hand. As Paul wrote to the Ephesians, "And he himself gave some to be apostles, some prophets, some evangelists, some pastors and teachers, equipping the saints for the work of ministry, to build up the body of Christ" (Eph 4:11).

As one considers this list, it is important to recognize everyone has an area of gifting. We are reminded of this in the Scriptures.

Just as each one has received a gift, use it to serve others, as good stewards of the varied grace of God. If anyone speaks, let it be as one who speaks God's Words; if anyone serves, let it be from the strength God provides, so that God may be glorified through Jesus Christ in everything. To him be the glory and the power forever and ever. Amen.

(1 Pet 4:10–11)

Just as there are millions of people who need to hear God's Word, there are also a sea of available ministry opportunities to complete this work. This is a broad list of many areas where God calls workers.

Where God Calls

Apologist

Association mission strategist

Biblical counselor

Bible teachers

Chaplain—Hospital, jail, military, police

Celebrate recovery pastor

Christian camp manager/staff member

Church planter

Church re-planter

Church reconciliation pastor/mediator

College campus ministry

Collegiate Gen Z pastor

Counselor—Addiction, children, divorce, grief, marriage

Discipleship pastor

Denominational leadership

Domestic missionary

Equipping Pastors—Pastors who mentor and encourage church leadership

Evangelist

Executive pastors—Oversee ministry teams in large churches

Foreign missionary

Homeless ministry

Marriage ministry leader

Media ministry

Member care ministry

Men's ministry

Missions pastors (local and regional missions)

Prison ministry

Seminary instructors

Senior Pastor—Inner city, suburban, rural

Senior adults ministry

Small groups pastor

Street ministry

Women's ministry leader

Worship pastor

Youth ministry

Where is God calling you?

How God Calls

There are many stories throughout the Scriptures describing how God calls men to service. This is especially seen throughout the Old Testament:

- In Genesis 12 God called Abraham to leave his homeland and become the father of a great nation.
- In Exodus 3 Moses encountered the Lord in the burning bush and was called to lead the Israelites from bondage in Egypt to the promised land.
- In 1 Samuel 3:1–10 the young Samuel distinctly heard the voice of God.
- In 1 Samuel 9–10 the Lord called Saul to be the first king of Israel, and he was anointed by the prophet Samuel.
- In 1 Samuel 16:12 God called David, the youngest of his brothers.
- God called his prophets (like Isaiah and Jeremiah), and he called Jonah to proclaim repentance to Nineveh.

God is still calling men and women to service yet today, although the roles vary between men and women—God clearly calls men to preach. It is fascinating to witness how God calls men to ministry in many different contexts, how they heard the voice of God, and how others confirmed their calling.

One such individual is Mac Lake. Mac grew up in a small West Virginia town and gave his life to Jesus at a young age. He experienced a strong pull to enter the ministry at the age of eighteen; he felt inadequate, but he had a strong stirring in his soul. He was encouraged by his mother and others who confirmed his calling. He served as pastor at Sea Coast Church in Myrtle Beach, South Carolina, and has been a strong influence in the church planting movement in the United States and leads the ministry Multiply Group.

Eddie Hancock serves as pastor at Crosspoint Church in Caldwell, Idaho. In relating his call to ministry testimony, he said, "It would have never started unless I went to youth camp when I was nineteen years old." Eddie said, "I got the sense that I had many friends who didn't know the Lord who would go to hell if they didn't meet him, and God was calling me to help them follow Jesus." Upon returning to his church and speaking to others, it became clear that he had a call to ministry to help people find Jesus and know him.

Jeremy Franks grew up in church and was at a revival meeting when he felt God called him. He said, "I wanted to know what God wanted me to do." Jeremy asked, "God what do you want me to do? And he very clearly said, 'Just trust me—just trust me!' And I knew in the moment God was calling me to ministry." Jeremy serves as the pastor at Fellowship Baptist Church in Morgan's Point Resort, Texas.

It is also important to realize the call to ministry maybe a process, as God is working in the life of a person over time to prepare them. Jose Marco is the pastor of Emmanuel Church in Madison, Wisconsin. Jose shared, "The discovery of the purpose of what God had for me took me a few years." He said, "in the meantime God was training me and equipping me to be ready." Jose moved from Argentina to the United States and is active in planting churches to reach the Latino community throughout his region.

David Gonzales shares in his story that his wife Amber introduced him to the gospel when they were dating in high school. She was a very instrumental influence upon encouraging him in his faith, along with prayers of others, and he came to Christ when he was twenty-three years old. His call to ministry became apparent to him as he grew up in the Catholic church and began to test the teachings of the Catholic Church and began to really search the Scriptures. He developed a love for God's Word and a desire to share it with others. David is the pastor at the First Baptist Church in Douglas, Arizona.

Sometimes a person feels they are called and ready to serve but must wait on God's timing. Matt Wunderlin's call-to-ministry story began more than twenty years ago while living in Los Angeles, California. He felt a real yearning for ministry and explains in his testimony it was not affirmed by the local church, not just once but a couple times. He related, by the providence of God and his timing and agreement of the church, he later was truly called into ministry. Matt serves as the pastor for Rolling Hills Church located in Platteville, Wisconsin. Matt also serves a Lt. Colonel in the United States Air Force Reserve.

Upon reflecting on the experiences of these men, the pattern for the call to ministry is very similar as God created a stirring in their hearts and a burning desire to share the love of Jesus. Their desire was witnessed by others and confirmed by the evidence of the Holy Spirit truly placing a call on their lives for ministry service to glorify Jesus.

Why the Urgency?

The Bible serves as a great mirror reflecting back to us the errors of humanity from ancient times until today. As we stare in this great mirror taking a glimpse of the past, we see a very similar reflection. In 2 Chronicles, we witness a similar environment to ours in the twenty-first century.

King Ahaz had steered his nation of Judah from living in godliness to worshiping false gods and even killing their children. Does this sound familiar? Upon his death, his son Hezekiah became the king of Judah at age twenty-five. King Hezekiah restored the temple and marshaled the efforts of the priests and Levites, commanding them to consecrate the temple and renew the covenant with the Lord so that God would not turn away from them. He said, and mind you, this is a twenty-five-year-old man, "My sons, don't be negligent now, for the Lord has chosen you to stand in his presence, to serve him and his ministers and burners of incense" (2 Chr 29:11). The purpose of sharing this narrative is today more than ever we need men to stand for truth, we need men to live holy lives, and we need men to minister and share the Word of God with the world.

In our world, according to statistics provided by Radical Ministries, "there are over 3.2 billion people unreached and without the gospel message. This makes up over seven thousand people groups."[14] As we focus on this hemisphere, particularly North America, according to the North American Mission Board, "there are over 281 million people who do not know Jesus."[15]

281 million equates to three out of four people in North America without a relationship with Christ. One more statistic to consider is a 2020 study conducted by Ligonier Ministries that reported: "52 percent of U.S. adults believe that Jesus is not God."[16]

Hezekiah's challenge in 729 BC still stands as a challenge for today's

---

[14] https://radical.net/article/great-commission-statistics-concern/accessed March 21st, 2025

[15] 2024 NAMB Ministry Report, https://www.namb.net/resource/2024-namb-ministry-report/accessed March 21st, 2025

[16] Ligonier.org, Is Jesus Divine?

men of faith. His challenge was for the priests to rise up and exalt the Lord. Similarly, we need men to rise up and tool up—praying, studying, and devouring God's Word and heralding it in the four corners, starting with our own communities. One must realize the need for Christ is everywhere, as even the Bible Belt has become a cultural ruin. It appears everyone is a Christian where I live on the north edge of Nashville in Sumner County, Tennessee. The county is situated in the heart of the Bible Belt with churches on nearly every street corner and around every curve along the roads. Yet, with a population of 208,182, there are still by all estimates 156,144 people who do not really know Jesus.

A major effort is needed share Christ. We need to improve the level of our discipleship, and we need more men to step up to proclaim the Word of God. The church is not dead, but if multiplication is to take place, real leadership within the church is required to mobilize Christians discipling believers to equip and embolden those who love Christ to evangelize the lost.

Where and How Is God calling You to Serve?

Thus far, we have considered where God is calling men and the many roles to be fulfilled, providing examples of those God has called and the urgency of sharing the gospel in our moment. It is also essential to understand that service to the Lord requires a genuine love for others.

A real desire to share the gospel message—I mean the kind that burns within your soul and seeps from your skin—must permeate your being. The apostles provide the best example of this innate desire to share Jesus with the world. Their witness is described in detail in the book of Acts.

It begins in Acts 2, when on the day of Pentecost Peter preached to the crowd outside the city wall of Jerusalem. He called them to repent and be baptized in the name of the Lord Jesus, and three thousand were added to the church. In Acts 6 Stephen was filled with the love of Jesus, and through the power of the Holy Spirit performed many signs and wonders. In Acts 8 Philip was proclaiming Jesus in Samaria, and in Acts 9 Saul was converted and immediately began proclaiming Jesus as the Messiah.

In our steeked American society, it seems so much easier to cower to the culture rather than be bold in one's witness. This is where the rubber meets the road for those wrestling with the call to ministry. In Acts 4 and

5 Peter and John were jailed, in Acts 7 Stephen was stoned, and in Acts 12 James was martyred. There are Christians today who die for their faith in other countries. Open Doors states thirteen people die for their faith every day.[17] The standing question truly for all Christians is, how strong is your faith?

In 1970 Lynn Anderson recorded the song "I Never Promised You a Rose Garden." Even though it's an oldie, the title of song is a phrase that remains pertinent today. Ministry is not a rose garden. Sadly, much of the challenge a ministry leader will face will be more external than internal. This is why it is essential to possess a genuine love for others and why it requires a sensitivity to understand and care for people. Develop your leadership skills to move the people of God where he is working and be a real light for those walking in darkness.

Stephen is a great example of a man who truly experienced the love of Jesus. In Acts 6:8 we learn that he was full of grace and power. His message to the Sanhedrin was amazing, as he was filled with the Holy Spirit and with the Word of God. His knowledge of the Word didn't happen instantaneously; he would have read the Scriptures and faithfully listened to many priests in the synagogues. This is a prime example of why my pastor, Robby Gallaty says, "You should get into the Word until the Word gets into you" and reverently sit under the authority of those who faithfully preach the Bible. Stephen knew the Word and was impacted by the gospel message so much that he could not contain himself. It was easy for him to be bold in his witness because he knew nothing else.

Consider these questions in your walk with Jesus: Do you feel the pull of the Holy Spirit fanning the flames of your faith so much so you cannot but help share Jesus with everyone you meet? Is Jesus imprinted in your DNA? Are those within your reach able to feel him, see him, and sense him in your words, actions, and habits? Are you truly able to put your "yes" on the table and say wherever and whatever?

We pray that you are and that you continue to grow where you've been planted. And as God grows you, may he bear the kind of fruit in your life that leads to righteousness so that you can best shepherd the flock that he has given to you.

---

[17] See more at https://www.opendoorsus.org/.

Chapter 3

Next Steps While You Wait

Tim LaFleur

See if this is you. You've felt what you believe is a call from the Lord into ministry leadership. You've spent time discerning that call and clarified that the call is genuine. But now you don't know where to go. You find yourself asking, "What can I do while I am in God's waiting room?"

We'll deal with that question, but before we do, there are a few principles that might apply to you as a sort of foundation for the steps that come next.

God Is Working While You Are Waiting

While you are waiting, God is working. In fact, he is working in at least two areas of your life. First, he is working to accomplish his overriding purpose in your life to make you more like Jesus. Notice what Paul says in his letter to the Romans:

We know that all things work together for the good of those who love God, who are called according to his purpose. For those he foreknew he also predestined to be conformed to the image of his Son, so that he would be the firstborn among many brothers and sisters. (Rom 8:28–29)

What an amazing promise! God is not only making all things "work together" for our good and for his glory, but he is making us more like Jesus.

The second way he is working is that he is "working out" his gracious providence in your life. He is working behind the scenes to accomplish his will and purpose for your life. And as you wait on him, he will "direct your path." Remember Proverbs 3:5–6:

Trust in the Lord with all your heart, and do not rely on your own understanding;

In all your ways know him, and he will make your paths straight.

In addition, while you are waiting, God may be preparing your spouse or children to step into a life of service through ministry leadership. So many men and women have not been able to pursue ministry leadership because their family was not on board. So, it is crucial that God works not only in your life but in their lives as well.

A Call to Ministry Is a Call to Prepare

When God calls someone to ministry leadership, he calls them to prepare. While waiting upon the Lord to show you the path he has for you, you can be intentional about your preparation.

I spent many years doing ministry in south Louisiana and was blessed to have rich fellowship with pastors in the Bayou. One of these men shared with us a truth that I have never forgotten. He said, "It's a whole lot easier for God to steer a moving vessel than one tied up to the dock." In other words, obey God in the things that you know he wants you to do, and as you are faithful to obey him in those things, he will reveal more of his will and purpose so that you can trust him and obey. I love what Proverbs 4:18 says: "The path of the righteous is like the light of dawn, shining brighter and brighter until midday."

While you are waiting, let me suggest several things that you can be intentional about doing that will help you to prepare to do the ministry God has called you to.

- Pursue spiritual growth.
- Connect with a local church.
- Seek out godly mentors.
- Gather with an accountability group (Above Reproach Group).
- Continue your education.

Pursue Spiritual Growth

The first step you should take while waiting on God is to pursue spiritual growth. A growing relationship with Christ is not optional; it is essential. Cultivating a deep, intimate relationship with Jesus should be the desire of every Christ follower but also and especially for those whom He's called to ministry leadership.

I love what the apostle Paul says in Philippians 3:10: "My goal is to know him and the power of his resurrection and the fellowship of his sufferings, being conformed to his death." The Amplified Bible begins verse 10 with, "for my determined purpose is to know Him." More than anything else Paul desires to know Christ, to have a deep intimate growing relationship with Jesus Christ!

How about you? Is that your desire—to know Christ more than anyone or anything else? While you wait on God for the next steps, cultivate your relationship with God so that you can discern his will and purpose for your life. Notice what the psalmist says:

> *No one who waits for you*
> *will be disgraced;*
> *those who act treacherously without cause*
> *will be disgraced.*
> *Make your ways known to me, Lord;*
> *teach me your paths.*
> *Guide me in your truth and teach me,*
> *for you are the God of my salvation;*
> *I wait for you all day long. (Ps 25:3–5)*

According to the psalmist, those who wait on the Lord will not "be disgraced." He goes on to say, "I wait for you all day long." This is a beautiful picture of his utter dependence upon God! He is resting in the grace of God and relying on the promises of God. While you wait on God, rest in him, being confident that as you grow spiritually he will reveal the next steps to you.

Primary Ways God Grows Us

In his book *Spiritual Disciplines for the Christian Life*, Donald Whitney shares that there are three catalysts God uses to grow us: people, circumstances, and the spiritual disciplines. He goes on to say, "We don't have any control on the people God brings into our lives or our circumstances, but we can be intentional about spending time with God through the spiritual disciplines."[18] In fact, Paul tells us to "train yourself in godliness" (1 Tim 4:7).

Do not see the spiritual disciplines as an end in themselves, but see them as a means to an end: to connect with God. As you spend time with God, you will learn more about his character, his purpose, and his ways. Notice 2 Corinthians 3:18: "We all, with unveiled faces, are looking as in a mirror at the glory of the Lord and are being transformed into the same image from glory to glory; this is from the Lord who is the Spirit." According to Paul, as you behold the Lord Jesus, you will be transformed into his image. And you will "behold him" by spending unhindered, uninterrupted time with him in his Word and prayer (along with the other spiritual disciplines).

Position Yourself to Receive from God

The late Jerry Bridges once said, "Sanctification is a work that God does, but it requires our effort."[19] I believe that "our effort" is to position ourselves to receive from God. You do that primarily by "abiding in Christ." Look at what Jesus says in John's Gospel: "Remain in me, and I in you. Just as a branch is unable to produce fruit by itself unless it remains on the vine, neither can you unless you remain in me. I am the vine; you are the branches. The one who remains in me and I in him produces much fruit, because you can do nothing without me" (John 15:4–5).

You must be intentional about abiding, continuing, and remaining in Christ. This is the key to spiritual health, growth, and fruitfulness. As you (a branch) abide in Jesus (the True Vine), he will supply all the resources you need for spiritual life and godliness. The key to an abundant life is

---

[18] Donald S. Whitney, *Spiritual Disciplines for the Christian Life* (Colorado Springs, CO: NavPress, 2014).

[19] Jerry Bridges, *Transforming Grace* (Colorado Springs: Tyndale Publishing House, 1991), 25.

to be vitally connected to Jesus. So, as you wait, pursue spiritual growth!

Connect with a Local Church

Notice what the writer of the book of Hebrews says in 10:24–25: "And let us consider one another in order to provoke love and good works, not neglecting to gather together, as some are in the habit of doing, but encouraging each other, and all the more as you see the day approaching" (Heb 10:24-25). Consider the phrase "not neglecting to gather together as some are in the habit of doing." Apparently, not being faithful to regularly attend the assembly of believers is not a new phenomenon. It was a problem in the early church as well.

Created for Community

As a new believer in Christ, the man who discipled me helped me understand that the Christian life was never meant to be lived alone. He taught me that the church was made up of the "called-out" ones. As Christ followers, we have been called out of the world and into fellowship with God and his people.

This is reflected in Acts 2. On the day of Pentecost, Peter is filled with the Holy Spirit and preaches the gospel. The Bible records that three thousand people came to faith in Christ and were baptized. Notice what Scripture says they were doing in Acts 2:42: "They devoted themselves to the apostles' teaching, to the fellowship, to the breaking of bread, and to prayer" (Acts 2:42). Also, notice what verses 46 and 47 say:

Every day they devoted themselves to meeting together in the temple, and broke bread from house to house. They ate their food with joyful and sincere hearts, praising God and enjoying the favor of all the people. Every day the Lord added to their number those who were being saved.

These believers were meeting corporately for worship and in small groups from house to house. Listen, God created you for community! If you are not a part of a local church, let me encourage you to identify with a local body of believers.

Get to Know the Pastor and Other Spiritual Leaders

As you are getting connected with the church, make it a priority to spend some time with the pastor and/or other spiritual leaders in the church to share what God is doing in your life. Set up an appointment with his assistant for lunch or coffee with the pastor rather than talking to him before or after services in the hallway. Because of the gravity of what God is doing in your life, it will be important to be able to share your story free from interruption.

If the pastor is unavailable during this season, perhaps he would suggest a staff member who could meet with you and encourage you. At any rate, godly pastors and staff members can be a valuable resource as you prepare for next steps. Why? Because they know what you are going through and can identify with what you are feeling and experiencing.

Volunteer for a Serve Team

One of the easiest and most practical steps you can take is to volunteer with a serve team. Many churches have spiritual gifts inventories that will help you discover your spiritual gifts. Also, what you are passionate about can also help you get to the "right" team. If the church is smaller, you may want to begin by talking with the pastor or lay leaders in the church to determine the right fit for you. This on-the-job training can be invaluable in discovering and developing your spiritual gifts and abilities.

Find Accountability

According to Webster, accountability is "the obligation to report, explain, or justify. To be responsible for or answerable to someone."[20] Practically speaking, accountable relationships can only happen when we give others permission to walk alongside us, observe our manner of life, and share with us the things that don't measure up to Christ.

At this point, some may push back and say, "Why do I need others when I am indwelled by the Holy Spirit?" While that is true, it is easy to

---

[20] *The Merriam-Webster Dictionary*, 11th ed. s.v. "accountability."

be deceived. We all have blind spots. We have talked ourselves into thinking that all is well when all the while we have harmful habits, destructive behaviors, or attitudes and actions that don't honor God. That is why we need trusted friends who love us enough to tell us the truth. That is why we all desperately need accountability!

Seek Godly Mentors

The first way that you can find the accountability that you will need during this pivotal time is to seek out godly mentors, men or women who walk with God and are pursuing him. These people have already walked down the path that you are embarking and will draw from their experience to provide wisdom and insight. They have already paid the "dumb tax" and can help you avoid pitfalls and see things from another perspective. As the Scripture says in Proverbs, "Without guidance, a people will fall, but with many counselors there is deliverance" (Prov 11:14).

When I was a college student at LSU, two men really helped me while trying to discern God's will concerning my calling: Frank Horton (my BSU director) and Don Tabb (pastor of the chapel on campus). These men ministered to me by serving as a sounding board, praying for me, and providing much-needed feedback. They always seemed to have "a word fitly spoken" and encouraged me to pursue God's calling on my life.

Join a Discipleship Group

In addition, I would encourage you to join a discipleship group or similar small group that will focus on spiritual growth and accountability. You will want to journey together with other men or women who are pursuing Christ and his calling on their lives. Notice what Proverbs 27:17 says: "Iron sharpens iron, and one person sharpens another." Those pursuing God's call on their lives and are trying to figure out next steps need people to journey with them to grow spiritually and hold one another accountable.

Seek Enrichment

Over the last several years, before my current assignment, I served two larger churches in Tennessee: Brainerd Baptist Church in Chattanooga and Long Hollow Church in Hendersonville. While serving there, I noticed that several men were wrestling with a call to ministry leadership and had no one to walk with them and serve as a sounding board or give them feedback. In addition, there were several younger men who were interns or on our staff that were new to the ministry and therefore lacked ministry experience. Several of the young men went to seminary online and never had a forum to discuss with others theology or concepts they were learning in their classes or from the books they were reading. As I observed all these things, I was prompted to begin what I called an "Above Reproach" group.

The name comes from 1 Timothy 3:2, where Paul lays out the qualifications of an elder:

"An overseer, therefore, must be above reproach, the husband of one wife, self-controlled, sensible, respectable, hospitable, able to teach." Notice that being "above reproach" is the first quality on the list. It seemed to be an appropriate name along, especially since so many men were leaving the ministry because their competency outran their character.

During the first group, we walked through the Pastoral Epistles, learned how to do inductive Bible study, learned the basic steps to the sermon, discussed hot topics in church life, talked about struggles, and prayed together.

When I went to Long Hollow, rather than doing one continuous group (with guys coming in and out), I took a semester approach with a beginning and ending time. This allowed us to have holidays and summers off. This is the approach that I would recommend.

Pastor, let me encourage you. When you have men who are wrestling with a call to ministry leadership, walk with them and provide feedback to help them follow the call that God has placed on their lives. Many of the men who have been in these groups with me are now in full-time ministry leadership and are choice servants of God. Pastor, I know that you are very busy, but let me encourage you to invest in these emerging leaders.

Continue Education

Some of you may feel led to pursue some sort of continuing education. There are so many things that you can take advantage of: conferences, seminars, online courses, master classes, a variety of podcasts, and YouTube channels. Others may want to pursue a more formal education by enrolling in Bible college or seminary. Let me encourage you to test the waters with a basic certificate or degree. I have had men in my Above Reproach groups who have gotten certificates from seminaries and also basic master's degrees such as master of Christian ministries. It is a good practice to make sure you seek enrichment while you are figuring out next steps.

Section 2
Timothy: His Life and Lessons in Leadership

Chapter 4

A Study on One Who Was Called

Rob Millman

One of the great privileges in life is to be mentored by an amazing teacher. One of the best biblical examples of mentoring is the relationship between the apostle Paul and Timothy.

Paul would have met Timothy for the very first time approximately in 50 AD, when Timothy was between twenty-two and twenty-three years of age. In Acts 16:2, Luke wrote the believers in both Lystra and Iconium spoke well of Timothy. According to Bible scholars, based on this information, Timothy would have traveled between both cities and developed relationships with the local people as they admired and commended him.

Nothing is mentioned of Timothy's father except that he was Greek. Therefore, he was mentored by his mother Eunice and Grandmother Lois (as noted in 2 Tim 1:5). Both women likely encountered Paul during his first missionary journey to Lystra in 46 AD. The account of this journey is noted in Acts 14.

It was during Paul and Barnabas's first visit to Lystra that a crippled man was healed by the power of God, and the locals mistook them for *gods*. They believed Barnabas to be Zeus and Paul to be Hermes. A local priest for these pagan gods brought a bull and wreathes to be sacrificed, and both Paul and Barnabas tore their clothes, explaining to the people they were not gods—but they knew of a *living* God to trust.

The Scriptures indicate they barely stopped the priests from sacrificing to them, and unbelieving Jewish men came from Antioch and Iconium who did not believe in Jesus as the Messiah. They won over the crowds, who rallied together and stoned Paul. Thinking he was dead, they dragged him out of the city.

The believing disciples gathered around Paul, and miraculously he got up went back into town, and then the next day he and Barnabas traveled to Derbe. They returned to Lystra to encourage and strengthen the believers and help them choose elders for the church. Paul and Barnabas left a lasting impression with the believers in Lystra, and their influence upon this church most likely strongly influenced Timothy's mother Eunice and his grandmother Lois.

During Paul's first visit to Lystra, Timothy would probably have been a teenager. He may have been a firsthand witness to Paul and Barnabas's ministry and stamped in his memory their dramatic resilience, creating a strong impression of God's hand upon their lives.

In Paul's second letter to Timothy, he wrote: "But as for you, continue in what you have learned and firmly believed. You know those who taught you, and you know that from infancy you have known sacred Scriptures, which are able to give you wisdom for salvation through faith in Christ Jesus" (2 Tim 3:14–15). Since Timothy's father was a Greek, a Gentile, he would have learned the Scriptures from his mother who was a Jewess. In the context of first-century Jewish tradition, a child began his religious training at age five and would continue until twelve or thirteen years of age. Evidently, Timothy's mother and grandmother provided him the traditional religious education necessary to be part of Jewish society.

As we reflect on this part of Timothy's life, there are couple of key points for reflection. The first point is to realize the significance of discipling children beginning at a young age. Timothy's mother and grandmother were a strong influence in the formation of his character and spiritual growth from the day he was born.

In today's society, we need to follow their example. In a 2020 Barna study entitled "Guiding Children," the following observation was noted: "Children who are most active in church tend to engage with the Bible outside of church, to attend church activities other than Sunday worship (such as Bible studies, camps or children's / youth events) and to pray together with their family as well. They are also about twice as likely to engage in outreach activities and volunteerism, demonstrating that the level of dedication in this group to the overall mission of the church is not only internally focused, but expresses itself in outward action."[21] This provides credence for church leaders to develop and sustain vibrant children's programs, especially since the likelihood to make a decision to follow Christ is greater at a young age.

Additionally, pastors need to identify men to shepherd. In Acts 16:3 we read that Paul chose Timothy. He was an obvious choice because he was active in the church exhibiting character and leadership traits. Timothy spoke not only Greek but the local Lycaonian language and perhaps was able to assist Paul and Silas to better communicate with others. Timothy was also spiritually prepared from his upbringing and most likely possessed a servant's heart and a moldable spirit to learn and grow. Paul chose him. The question for today's church leaders is, who are you choosing to grow and develop in your spiritual leadership pipeline?

A New Beginning

In Acts 16 Timothy begins a new chapter in his life as Paul witnessed in him traits essential to propagate the gospel message. He possessed the necessary disposition and temperament. His obedience is first observed in his willingness to be circumcised as to be more accepted by those with a Jewish background. This would grant his entrance into the Jewish synagogues; therefore, his submission was helpful. This is lesson one: "God only gives out assignments when we have the character to match it."[22]

The elders in the church of Lystra and Derbe knew Timothy's character, and God chose in his timing the next step for his spiritual journey: Paul ordained Timothy into service, as noted in 1 Timothy 4:14. A reminder to busy pastors, especially in a larger church, is to pay attention to your elders. Through their more intentional interaction and observation, they may know of a Timothy in your midst, a godly man possessing a love for Jesus, a passion for souls, and compassion for the lost.

As Timothy embarks on his journey with Paul, it really began years earlier from lessons learned in childhood. It was a culmination of lessons that developed his character. Timothy's spiritual education undoubtedly was

---

[21] "58% of Highly Engaged Christian Parents Choose a Church with the Kids in Mind," Barna, January 30, 2020, https://www.barna.com/research/children-church-home/, accessed July 13, 2023.

[22] Bob Burton, *The Spiritual DNA of a Church on Mission* (Nashville: B&H, 2020), 59.

accelerated each and every day in his travels, as Paul and Silas mentored him in the knowledge of God through the Word, their conversations, engagements, and interactions with those they met.

Those seeking God's will for their life can learn a valuable lesson here also: engage in a mentoring relationship with others. This is why a group designed for discipleship and accountability is so vital. It provides a safe place to interact with others, grow in faith, and to be mentored and strengthened.

Pastors, don't forget the significance of this process for your own spiritual growth. Paul brought Timothy along to be of service—not just to the ministry but to Paul himself. In the spirit of his example, today's pastors should also identify men and raise them up for service. These leaders, young and old, can assist a pastor in spiritual work based upon their skill sets. This system of leadership allows men to grow spiritually through active participation in the areas of member care, discipleship, and evangelism.

This was Paul's second missionary journey as these three men took the gospel message to Philippi, Thessalonica, Berea, Athens and Corinth. For Timothy as a young man, this would have been quite the adventure. Imagine the excitement and conversations while sailing from Troas across the Aegean Sea to Neapolis and then to Philippi. This young man raised in the faith, commissioned to accompany the apostle Paul himself, would have been absolutely on fire for the mission at hand.

This is where the Scriptures pick up their encounter with Lydia. Since there was not a Jewish synagogue there, the men on this missionary journey went outside the city along a nearby river to find a place to pray. There they encountered a group of women and spoke to them, and upon hearing the gospel message Lydia and her whole household were baptized. This makes a good point for modern Christians: make an impact wherever you are. You do not need to have what most consider perfect conditions for worship; God is with you everywhere.

We can only conjecture about what happened next: that while Paul and Silas were encountering the crowd in Philippi, Paul may have sensed danger and, to protect Timothy, sent him away. Perhaps Timothy could have still been ministering to individuals they met along the river. This is what we do know: Paul had a paternal affinity toward Timothy and in the situation in Philippi would have been protective of him. Paul and Silas were beaten with rods, thrown in jail, and then be set free through God's providence.

So later, when Paul was imprisoned in Rome, he wrote back to Timothy in 2 Timothy 1:7: "for God has not given us a spirit of fear, but one of power, love and sound judgment." As one discerns the call to ministry, realize it will not always be easy, but you will never be alone. God qualifies and guides those he calls, and God has a calling for you.

One Who Honors God

The meaning of Timothy's name is "one who honors God," which perfectly frames the distinctive nature of his character. It is noted throughout his ministry that he persevered in his diligence to emulate Paul and serve him well. He proclaimed the gospel message in difficult environments and places where it required him to remain steadfast to the faith and to endure in the face of struggles. These basic attributes—perseverance, proclamation of the gospel, and endurance—are as relevant today as they were two millennia ago when Paul mentored Timothy. Today's church in North America is on the brink, as 281 million people do not know Jesus. This means that we pastor churches in a time with circumstances that feel similar to what Paul and Timothy encountered in Corinth. In his first letter to the Corinthians, Paul wrote the following:

> *For you may have countless instructors in Christ, but you don't have many fathers. For I became your father in Christ Jesus through the gospel. Therefore, I urge you to imitate me. This is why I have sent Timothy to you. He is my dearly loved and faithful child in the Lord. He will remind you about my ways in Jesus Christ, just as I teach everywhere in every church. (2 Cor 4:15–17)*

Paul knew he could count on Timothy to be a strong leader, and much like Paul, Timothy also was a father in Christ to many. Timothy also would shepherd the Corinthians and later the church in Ephesus. It was not an easy job, as the church encountered dysfunction dealing with immorality, lawsuits between believers, challenges with marriage, and many other struggles. Pastors today face these same situations, with which they must interact while displaying a high degree of integrity, understanding, and solid people skills. Brian Croft, the author of *Biblical Church Revitalization*, lists the essential qualities and abilities today's pastor must possess:

- Visionary shepherd
- High tolerance for pain
- Respect and passion for the church's legacy
- Passion for multi-generational ministry
- A resourceful generalist
- Tactical patience
- Emotional awareness
- Spousal perseverance[23]

As one discerns his call to ministry, he must assess his personal nature to fulfill the role of a pastor to shepherd others. A man must evaluate his character to be a servant of Jesus Christ, to remain true to the Word, to be strong in grace, and he must realize the struggle is real. There will be attacks from within and without.

Timothy faced both of these as he pastored the church in Ephesus. It requires spiritual strength and unwavering belief in the purity of the gospel message. Timothy was Paul's coworker and his traveling companion. Together they shared the gospel throughout the Macedonian region. Paul knew him well, schooled him, and treated him like his son. Because of his strong relationship and knowing the depth of his character, Paul entrusted Timothy to fulfill God's will and purpose in the church.

As a man considers his purpose and calling to ministry, it is the perfect time for introspection and reflection to evaluate the strength of his faith and how God desires to use them during his time on this earth. In 1729 John Wesley and his brother Charles formed the Holy Club at Christ Church in Oxford. The club included George Whitefield and others who met for prayer, Bible study, and reflection and accountability. They developed a list of twenty-two questions to ask themselves during private devotion. Here is a sampling of four questions from this list to consider as you contemplate your call to ministry: Can I be trusted? When did I last speak to someone about my faith? Do I disobey God in anything? Is Christ real to me?

---

[23] Brian Croft, *Biblical Church Revitalization* (Glasgow: Christian Focus, 2016), 34.

Based upon the Scriptures, it is evident Timothy could provide solid answers for all of these questions. Paul trusted him implicitly to herald the gospel, to pastor, and to minister to others. He obviously shared his faith with many. Christ was very real to him as witnessed in Paul's testimony calling him "my true son in the faith." How do your answers stack up?

Leading in God's House

In Paul's letter to the Philippians, he wrote:

Now I hope in the Lord Jesus to send Timothy to you soon so that I too may be encouraged by news about you. For I have no one else like-minded who will genuinely care about your interests; all seek their own interests, not those of Jesus Christ. But you know his proven character, because he has served with me in the gospel ministry like a son with a father. (Phil 2:19–22)

One of the hallmarks of leader is to trust those whom he leads to share the same values, transmit the same message, care for others with the same level of empathy, and express the highest-level character and service to those whom they serve. Paul mentored Timothy on their many travels and knew his character well. Timothy was true to the faith and likeminded to his teacher. For these reasons, Paul left for Macedonia after leaving Timothy to lead the church in Ephesus. It was during this time Paul wrote his first letter to Timothy to encourage him. Some biblical scholars state the main crux of this letter is reflected in the third chapter:

But if I should be delayed, I have written so that you will know how people ought to conduct themselves in God's household, which is the church of the living God, the pillar and foundation of truth. (1 Tim 3:15)

It could be said this key verse encapsulates the entire message of Paul's first letter to Timothy. Paul's desire was to provide practical information for Timothy to oversee the Ephesian church. The church is the house of the living God; he is the ruler of the church, he is the architect and the builder of the church, and he lives there and provides for it.

The Ephesian church was not without its woes, as false doctrine was prevalent and the law was misused. Paul instructed Timothy to fight the good fight, and he noted that some had shipwrecked their faith by believing in false teachings. It cannot be overstated that in our modern times, today's leaders in the church—pastors, preachers, and teachers—must possess spiritual strength and unwavering belief in the purity of the gospel message. Paul mentions the false teachers Hymenaeus and Alexander in 1:20. Our culture today is also not without false teachers who are very convincing in their delivery and methods to lure away and sway people off track. This is why strong leadership is imperative to proclaim the truth.

Sadly, in our society there are preachers standing in pulpits who are deceivers preaching many false gospels. Consider some of these false gospels:

- The religion gospel, which says you are saved by your good works.
- The moralism gospel, which says that if you are a good person, God will let you into heaven.
- The self-help gospel, which teaches that God will help you live your best life now.
- The sign and wonders gospel, which says if you are really saved, you will see miracles.

And there are more: the therapeutic gospel, the social justice gospel, and the prosperity gospel, just to name a few.

Is your gospel *The* Gospel? The one that is centered around the person, death, and resurrection of Jesus? We are to preach only the truth. We are saved by grace through faith in our Lord Jesus Christ because he was nailed to the cross to pay for our sins and redeem us by taking our place and reconciling us to the Father! This is the truth Paul entrusted to Timothy and charged him to teach.

Paul wrote in his letter to the Galatians: "But even if we or an angel from heaven should preach to you a gospel contrary to what we have preached to you, a curse be on him. As we have said before, I now say again: If anyone is preaching to you a gospel contrary to what you received, a curse on him!" (Gal 1:8–9).

God's house is the pillar and foundation of truth and it is important for a man seeking God's will to follow through on his call to study and know the Word. A man must seek the truth and ground himself. It is essential as one discerns a calling to ministry to have strong spiritual mentors and an eagerness to learn and advance one's studies. Paul's protégé Timothy is a solid example of how men today should remain steadfast to the true gospel message, stand firm in the face of trials, and preach truth.

Wholehearted Devotion

Timothy possessed an unfeigned devotion to God. His faith was genuine and authentic; he was dedicated to the truth. Timothy willingly followed Paul as God's servant, knowing what happened in Lystra, and was willing to accept the hardships of being a true follower of Christ. Paul took a great liking to Timothy and developed a strong paternal relationship with him. Paul's two letters to Timothy have throughout the ages become well-known as part of Pastoral Epistles, along with the book of Titus. The letters were written to provide Timothy comfort, strength, and instruction on how to properly manage the church. The followers of Jesus were still a fledging group of believers, and some were off course in their beliefs. Paul wrote these letters to Timothy to provide direction and bolster his diligence to steady the church.

In his first letter, Paul reminded Timothy to be an example in his speech, love, faith, and purity (1 Tim 4:12). Timothy had been ordained by the laying on of hands: "Don't neglect the gift that was in you; it was given to you through prophecy and the laying on of hands by the council of elders" (1 Tim 4:14). Paul also wrote good advice for Timothy and believers today, especially those who are leaders and contemplating service in ministry leadership: "Pay close attention to your life and your teaching; persevere in these things for in doing this you will save both you and your hearers" (1 Tim 4:16).

Second Timothy is the final letter written by Paul as he himself was in the midst of a trial, and it was apparent to him that his fate was dire. He urged Timothy to remain faithful to him. There were other believers who doubted Paul's true apostleship since he was imprisoned so much, but still Paul urged Timothy not to be ashamed of the gospel and to remain loyal to the faith by holding onto a pattern of sound teaching (1:13). In the second chapter of this letter, Paul shared three examples of faithfulness: a soldier, an athlete, and a farmer, suggesting to Timothy to commit to something greater to accomplish the Lord's work. He also reflected on Jesus's crucifixion and his own imprisonment, which illustrate how following Christ requires endurance. Look at how Paul wrote about enduring with devotion to Jesus:

> *This saying is trustworthy: For if we died with him, we will also live with him; if we endure, we will also reign with him; if we deny him, he will also deny us; if we are faithless, he remains faithful, for he cannot deny himself. (2 Tim 11–13)*

Paul directed Timothy to be an approved worker, a man who pursues righteousness, faith, love, and peace, calling on the Lord with a pure heart (1:27). He encouraged Timothy to guard himself from those who engage in empty speech, to be gentle instead of quarrelsome so that perhaps God may grant them repentance. In chapter 3, Paul reminded Timothy that all Scripture is God-breathed: "All Scripture is inspired by God and is profitable for teaching, for rebuking, for correcting, for training in righteousness, so that the man of God may be complete, equipped for every good work" (2 Tim 3:16–17).

In the final chapter of this letter, Paul encouraged Timothy to "Preach the word; be ready in season and out of season; rebuke, correct, and encourage with great patience and teaching" (2 Tim 4:2). Paul provided a charge to Timothy to be bold, to preach the truth of the gospel even though he, too, may suffer. He wanted to make Timothy aware that people turned away from Paul for preaching truth, and he wanted Timothy to clearly understand they would also turn away from him.

Paul encouraged Timothy to visit him in prison and to bring him his cloak—a sleeveless garment worn for warmth that he had left in Troas—as well as the scrolls and parchments. These may have included some of his writing supplies and Hebrew Scriptures. It is not known if Timothy made his way to Rome to fulfill this request.

What else is known about Timothy's life is he was imprisoned, as the writer of Hebrews mentioned he had been released in 13:23. Tradition has it that Timothy was martyred in Ephesus when he was over eighty years old. There is not a clear explanation as how Timothy exactly died; however, the apocryphal of Acts of Timothy states that he attempted "to put an end to a pagan festival to honor Dionysus of Katagogion, in which the participants would dress in costumes, masks and partake in sexual immorality and murder. It was recorded that Timothy exhorted them saying, 'Men of Ephesus do not be mad for idols, but acknowledge the one who truly is God.' Instead of listening to Timothy revelers attacked and beat him. While Timothy was still barely alive, some fellow Christians took him away from the mob, and when he died, they buried him in a place call Pion in Ephesus."[24]

Like Paul, Timothy fought the good fight and finished the race well. His devotion was not counterfeit at all; it consumed his whole heart. May our lives be the same.

---

[24] https://www.gotquestions.org/how-did-Timothy-die.html, accessed August 6th, 2023.

Section 3
Mentoring Emerging Leaders

Chapter 5

How to Relate to a Man God Can Shape

ROB MILLMAN

Identifying Emerging Leaders

One of the key elements to identifying emerging leaders for ministry is to develop an attitude of intentionality. It requires a pastor or ministry leader to realize the importance of becoming acutely aware of those who show interest in learning and growing in their faith, as well as who have a deep desire to serve others. These individuals may be young men from pre-teen to twenty-somethings who have an interest in growing in the knowledge of the faith and seeking opportunities to serve, hoping to be asked. It could be a man who in their thirties, forties, or fifties who realizes they desire to contribute more to the advancement of the kingdom; it could even be older men who want to finish their lives well.

It is important to have an open-mindedness, realizing God doesn't necessarily call what we think is our ideal man. Consider Moses, as recorded in Stephen's message from Acts 7. Moses was forty years old when he went to visit the Israelites. Forty years later, an angel appeared to him from a burning bush. Therefore, Moses was eighty years old—and God had a plan for him. Don't be afraid to freshen up your mindset and keep your eyes open for those whom God considers to be workers for the expansion of his kingdom.

Although you probably want to encourage everyone in the church to be a multiplying disciple maker, the reality is there will only be a few who have a sense of calling for ministry leadership. Matthew recorded Jesus's words in Matthew 9:37–38: "Then he said to his disciples, 'The harvest is abundant, but the workers are few. Therefore, pray to the Lord of the harvest to send out workers into his harvest.'" Keeping this Scripture in mind provides clarity and also a charge to act upon Jesus's command as a good first step and pray for workers.

Do what you can to eliminate barriers to naturally occurring opportunities for one-on-one engagement. These special times could be after a worship service or in between meetings. If you catch yourself in a conversation, invite that person to breakfast. If you have a few people in mind, ask if they'd like to grab coffee once a week to connect about opportunities to serve others, pray, provide feedback, and hold one another accountable. Perhaps invite a small group of men to be actively engaged in a weekly discipleship group, reading through a Bible reading plan, memorizing Scripture, and providing time for accountability and prayer. All these ideas allow for moments of intimacy to assist a man to discern the will of God for his life and provide direction.

Persevere with patience! Spiritual growth and discernment take time. In our day and age of instant gratification, it is imperative to realize the process of shaping men into instruments God can use for his purpose is based upon his schedule. P. J. Tibayan, who pastors in Bellflower, California, noted, "We can't microwave faithfulness. Many still try, to their own disappointment and frustration. When we lack the perspective that growth and maturity take time, we give up too hastily on others and are drawn to the 'missing secret' of effective ministry."[25] As a pastor becomes intentional in his desire and ability to mentor emerging leaders, the beauty of gospel and the desire to herald the message will reveal itself within the hearts in those who are truly called.

A pastor who intentionally identifies and develops men on a consistent basis creates a process to raise up leaders in the church. These men can assist a pastor with making visits to the sick and shut-ins, teach classes, lead small groups, and be given opportunities to preach in

---

[25] P.J. Tibayan, "On Raising Men for Ministry: Lessons from a Former Solo Pastor," *Desiring God*, October 30, 2021, https://www.desiringgod.org/articles/on-raising-men-for-ministry, accessed April 10, 2023.

smaller venues offered by the church. This type of leadership process on behalf of a pastor will also provide a positive witness to everyone in the church on how to disciple others and raise up leaders. It also creates an environment for men who may be less distinctive or identifiable to church leaders to be more confident in their willingness to approach the pastor about their sense of calling.

The greatest joy a pastor can experience is multiplying leaders in the church. It is a great privilege to raise up men, watch them grow in their faith and abilities to advance the gospel, strengthen discipleship within the church, and reach the lost as God's instrument to change the world.

Praying for Workers

One of my favorite memories as a young boy visiting my grandparents on their farm in northern Indiana is flying kites with my siblings. My grandparents had a large field just beyond their chicken houses that offered plenty of open space to get a kite up high up in the air, and I remember our excitement when the kites were at their highest point, using every inch possible on the ball of string. Of course, there were times we wanted to fly our kites but there was no breeze. We would run as fast as we could, thinking we could catch an updraft, yet without the wind they were unable to fly and tumbled to the ground. How many times do we as Christians seek God, trying to do things in our own power, and all the sudden whatever it is, it just doesn't seem to work and, like the kite, we are grounded. There is no wind to power our prayer request, whatever it may be.

Flying a kite without wind is a great analogy as we consider praying for workers for the harvest field. As we meet with men and women of all ages who have an interest in ministry work, one of the obvious requirements is the power of a fresh wind from the Holy Spirit. The way we connect with the Holy Spirit is to get on our knees and seek God in prayer.

As twenty-first century Christians, we can take a cue from E. M. Bounds, who felt called to ministry in his early twenties during the Third Great Awakening and preached in the late 1800s. He wrote in his book *Power through Prayer* that "What the Church needs today is not more machinery or better, not new organization or more and novel methods, but men whom the Holy Ghost can use—men of prayer, men mighty in prayer. The Holy Ghost does not flow through methods, but through men. He does not come on machinery, but on men. He does not anoint plans, but men—men of prayer."[26]

Clearly, we seek the anointing of the Holy Spirit to anoint our efforts, and especially those with whom we pray to share the gospel message. Prayer has always been paramount, since the days of Old Testament heroes, and is now the key for us to seek the power of Holy Spirit to raise up emerging leaders for the work of the church.

A good first step as we prepare to pray is to make sure our thoughts are in step with Holy Spirit. Paul wrote In Romans 12:2, "Do not be conformed to this age, but be transformed by the renewing of your mind, so that you may discern what is the good, pleasing, and perfect will of God." In today's age, there appears no way to escape the world in the advent of a phone in our pocket, 24/7 news, social media, and all the other electronic mediums to keep us connected to the world. When we view social media, our minds are inundated with information and images that may not always be so godly.

Perhaps we spend too much time connected to the world when instead we should use every resource possible to be connected to God. Prayer provides that connection. As we renew our minds and consider what is good in the eyes of God, what is pleasing in his sight, and seek to live out his perfect will, we realize all the sudden that we are not to be part of this world. You see, the world only wants to take us places where man can be glorified rather than our Lord Jesus Christ. That is why as we prepare to pray for men to be raised up as pastors, we need to cleanse our thoughts, turn away from the world, and choose to be 100 percent in his presence.

Please pray for God to affect the hearts of men and women to call them to do his work in ministry to advance his kingdom. We pray especially for young men to be raised up into this high calling, and we pray for those who are older to consider the direction of their lives and how God can use their experiences, knowledge, and insight to impact the world with his Word. In the same mindset as that of the apostle Paul, we pray for men to do the work of ministry so the church may be unified and we grow into maturity in the knowledge of our Lord and Savior Jesus and proclaim his Word to the ends of the earth.

---

[26] E. M. Bounds, *Power through Prayer*, (New York: Marshall Brothers, 1912), 10.

Listening to the Voice of God

"Then he said to his disciples, "The harvest is abundant, but the workers are few. Therefore, pray to the Lord of the harvest to send out workers in his harvest" (Matt 9:37–38). Jesus shared these words with his disciples when walking among the crowds of people and possessing a deep compassion for them. He likened them to like sheep without a shepherd and urged his disciples to pray for ministry workers. Just as Jesus had a deep compassion for others, we too should possess hearts of benevolence. We are to take action and pray for workers and encourage those considering ministry as a vocation to pray for discernment and direction.

As we pray to God, we heighten our sense of awareness, and we cause ourselves to become more observant of those in our midst who exhibit the attributes, strengths, and heart for ministry. Through our prayers for God to work, we begin to see him demonstrate his work in the hearts and minds of others. This is where we begin to witness the evidence of God's work through our prayers and how he speaks. It is important to realize God may be speaking through you!

Paul wrote in Romans 12:6–8, "According to the grace given to us, we have different gifts: If prophecy, use it according to the proportion of one's faith; if service, use it in service; if teaching, in teaching; if exhorting, in exhortation; giving, with generosity; leading, with diligence; showing mercy, with cheerfulness." God speaks through his Scripture, and he speaks through preachers and teachers whose source is his Word. This is why it is essential for pastors and teachers to regularly call for ministry workers. It requires responsible leadership to grow the church and to stir the hearts of fellow disciples to consider ministry. This is an essential part of the leader's assignment—to inspire and to share the Savior's desire to send out workers into the harvest. As a leader speaks, a hearer listens; as a hearer listens to the Scripture, he doesn't necessarily hear the speaker but the voice of God. This is why a teacher should teach and a preacher should preach to herald his Word—so the voice of Jesus may be heard. And, as a hearer listens, he realizes God needs him, God needs him as a worker, he needs him to go!

As one heralds the Word from a pulpit, teaches in the classroom, or engages in one-on-one conversation, God is at work. He speaks through his Holy Spirit. Jesus explained this concept to his followers when he said in John 14:26, "but the Counselor, the Holy Spirit, whom the Father will send in my name, will teach you all things and remind you of everything I have told you." The Holy Spirit speaks through the Word, causing the heart of a believer to be impacted to acknowledge the great need required for the harvest causing the hearer to say, "Yes!"

We see this exact thing happen in Acts 13:2, where Luke recorded, "As they were worshiping the Lord and fasting, the Holy Spirit said, "Set apart for me Barnabas and Saul for the work to which I have called them." The work of the Holy Spirit was evidenced in the lives of not only Paul and Barnabas but also the men worshiping, fasting, and praying. The impact of the Holy Spirit was not only upon the two men to go, however. The impact also included the senders, who no doubt—although not recorded—must have prayed many prayers and poured wisdom and knowledge into Paul and Barnabas. They would have listened to the men, but more importantly to the Holy Spirit.

So what about you? Who has God placed upon your path? Is there a man or multiple men who possess special qualities or hold a desire in their heart that is so clear, so evident, that it is undeniable God is calling them? It is important to be mindful that God doesn't call the equipped but equips the called. As a leader, like the men noted in Acts 13:1 who prayed for Paul and Barnabas, be cognizant to listen, listen to others, yes, but most importantly, listen to the Holy Spirit.

Isaiah experienced the presence of the Lord in the temple, as noted in Isaiah 6:8, where the Lord called Isaiah and he listened. "Then I heard the voice of the Lord asking: Who should I send? Who will go for us? I said: Here I am. Send me." In 1868 Daniel March wrote these words in a hymn that echo Isaiah's response:

> *Hark! the voice of Jesus crying,*
> *"Who will go and work today?*
> *Fields are white and harvests waiting,*
> *Who will bear the sheaves away?"*
> *Loud and long the Master calleth,*
> *Rich reward He offers thee;*
> *Who will answer, gladly saying,*
> *"Here am I, send me, send me!"*

What is God calling you to do? Who is God placing in your life so that they, too, can hear God's voice and respond with faithfulness?

Providing Advice and Direction

In their book *Calling out the Called*, Pruitt and Pace strongly urge ministry leaders to give an invitation to call out the called. They preface by suggesting, "Pray, pray, and pray some more. You are desperately in need of the Lord to speak through you in a way that pierces hearts."[27] There are many individuals whom the Lord is calling that needs strong prayer to break them free and shape their hearts for surrendering to God's purpose for their life.

A great example of this is Carl Love's ministry-call experience. He now serves as the pastor of Transformation Community Church located in Temple, Texas. As a young man Carl made a decision to choose Jesus and attended a small church with his wife. He became actively involved, and one Sunday he felt compelled to come forward during the invitation at the end of service and chose not to do it. As he described his experience, he felt perhaps he needed to repent again, when in reality the Holy Spirit was working in his heart. In his description of his story, he felt the desire to come forward on two more occasions.

Finally, he met with his pastor and shared his experience. His pastor advised to go home, pray, and ask God what he wants him to do. So, Carl got on his face and prayed, and it was not long after he began to pray that he knew God was calling him to preach. As Pruitt and Pace shared, as a pastor, "You are desperately in need of the Lord to speak through you in way that pierces hearts."[28]

In Carl's case, he knew the Holy Spirit was working in his heart, and he went to see his pastor privately. This brings up the point it may be a good practice to prioritize having a special time set aside to meet with individuals who are wrestling with the call of the Lord on their lives. When shepherding young men, once they have confirmed they feel called and have a sincere desire to serve, they will have many questions. It may be good to meet on an ongoing basis to share insights, address questions, and provide answers on a personal level.

---

[27] Pace and Shane Pruitt, *Calling Out the Called*, 170.

[28] Pace and Shane Pruitt, *Calling Out the Called*, 170.

This is best done in an intimate setting rather than a large gathering. Consider getting men who are wrestling with their call together on an ongoing basis. This group could consist of only one or two men or a dozen—whatever makes it easiest for you to invest in them and provide guidance about steps required for training. In a setting like this, iron will sharpen iron, discernment will be cultivated, and the men you are mentoring will be challenged to think about the call through digesting and commenting on assigned reading. These assignments provide opportunities to grow in their knowledge but also a time to pray for one another. It will be a safe place for pastors to give advice and initiate an accountability process to give those participating the ability to grow deeper in their spiritual walk.

One of the best places for pastors to give great advice is in the Sunday morning pulpit, preaching each week to stir hearts that the Holy Spirit is shaping. As in Carl's experience, he felt the pull, but it took more than one experience, and his call wasn't necessarily based upon emotion but a real invitation. This is why it is essential to invite men and women who may be wrestling with the call to ministry to come forward on an ongoing basis. Each time they hear the invitation, through the work of the Holy Spirit, they hear the voice of God calling.

In addition to forming small groups and exhorting from the pulpit, you also have the opportunity to lead by example. Live a godly life, be a model of faith, and reflect the Word that is taught. The writer of Hebrews offers this advice for both leaders and followers: "Remember your leaders who have spoken God's word to you. As you carefully observe the outcome of their lives, imitate their faith" (Heb 13:7). As a practice of providing direction, nothing stands out more than being a great example as God's servant.

Shepherding is a huge responsibility, and investing in men for ministry is a key attribute of a thriving church. These men will aid and help sustain your ministry and empower your church to make a kingdom impact in your community now and in the future.

Empowering Emerging Leaders

Do you remember when you first learned how to drive a car? You could read the manuals and handbooks, you could watch videos, but nothing could replace the experience of being behind the wheel. The same holds true for future pastors and emerging leaders: nothing is more paramount than real-world experience, and it requires today's church leaders to provide opportunities.

When you first started to drive, you learned best through practical experience. Similarly, as a man of God grows in faith through reading and learning, he accelerates his growth when he "hits the road," so to speak! This is where the role of a pastor as mentor can provide additional opportunities for these men to discern their call when interacting with others.

Mark Dever, pastor of Capitol Hill Baptist Church in Washington, DC, believes you must advance trust in men to grow them for the ministry. He writes, "You probably have members of your church whom the Lord has entrusted with great talent. But for that to be discovered, someone must advance trust to them, like credit. And good leaders do this. They don't wait for people to prove themselves, and then give them teaching opportunities. No, they see the hint of something that, with a little encouragement, could grow and flourish."[29]

I remember when one of my pastors asked me years ago to organize a National Day of Prayer event for the local community. He gave me the hint, and I organized and led the effort for a decade. Years later, another pastor planted the seeds that led me to the opportunity to preach. My friend Kevin Lowhorn was given an opportunity to help lead a prayer ministry and has been called as an associate pastor at another church in a different state. I think about Buddy Toon who served on the police force for many years and felt a calling to come alongside side men who struggle with a multitude of issues due to the nature of their work. With encouragement, he now serves as a chaplain helping officers and also families and individuals in crisis situations. As noted, our pastors saw a little something within us and provided encouragement. A pastor is to be an encourager, which is vital to equip men for the ministry.

So how does the pastor encourage? It requires an investment in men. As Christians, we always think about Paul as Timothy's mentor, but sometimes we forget he himself was mentored by Barnabas. In Acts 11:22–26 Barnabas sought out Paul and brought him to Antioch where, for a whole year, he was able to mentor him. "Barnabas guided Paul during

---

[29] Mark Dever, "9 Ways to Raise Up Leaders in Your Church," *The Gospel Coalition*, June 5, 2017, https://www.thegospelcoalition.org/article/9-ways-to-raise-up-leaders-in-your-church/, accessed May 8, 2023.

his development from a novice follower of Christ to the greatest propagator of the faith in the early church. Senior leaders today can follow the example of Barnabas and contribute to the development of the next generation of leaders."[30]

Leaders are developed when provided tools, know-how, and most importantly opportunities. It is essential for pastors to embrace emerging leaders, providing encouragement and cracking open doors for men to grow in their faith and abilities. Paul wrote that some were called "to equip the saints for the work of ministry to build up the body of Christ" (Eph 4:12). This is where a smaller focused group of men is a great tool to provide a dynamic where different types of people come together to grow in their faith, strengthen their abilities, and sharpen their senses to discover their own gifts and reveal the talents of others. It is a place of prayer, brotherhood, and learning. It is a place where a pastor can have intimate conversation of discovery similar to those between Barnabas and Paul. It doesn't require a seminary environment but only a dedicated shepherd committed to equipping men of God to share the love of Jesus through the gospel message to a desperate and dying world.

As you consider this type of residency-building program to empower others in your church, there are plenty of opportunities for men to serve. They can lead small groups and discipleship groups, teach classes, deliver Sunday evening messages, assist with youth and adult ministries, organize community outreach programs, engage in mission work, and the list is endless. Empowering emerging leaders requires intentionality, it requires a servant's heart, and most importantly it requires true love for Jesus and embracing his desire to share the gospel with the world.

---

[30] Orlando Rivera, "Mentoring Stages in the Relationship between Barnabas and Paul," *Journal of Biblical Perspectives in Leadership* (2007): https://www.regent.edu/journal/journal-of-biblical-perspectives-in-leadership/mentoring-stages-in-the-relationship-between-barnabas-and-paul/, access May 8, 2023.

Chapter 6

Mentoring Emerging Leaders

Tim LaFleur

One of the greatest privileges is to disciple or mentor emerging leaders who feel they've been called to ministry leadership. And yet, few pastors and church leaders take advantage of that wonderful opportunity.

When people share that God is dealing with them about a call to ministry leadership, we normally say to ourselves, "These individuals are feeling called to ministry, so let's send them off to seminary." This is unfortunate because according to Barna Research, only 17 percent of evangelicals have had a godly mentor in their lives.[31] This thinking is neither biblical nor practical.

It is the responsibility of leaders in the local church to disciple and mentor those called to ministry leadership. After they have affirmed God's calling, they can then go to seminary for specialized training, but higher education should not replace the valuable relationship between a mentor and a mentee.

So many practical things can be experienced by emerging leaders in the local church as they are discipled and mentored by their local church leaders. This is invaluable preparation and training that you can't reproduce in a classroom setting.

A mentor, by definition, is a trusted counselor, a guide, a tutor, or a coach. I'm so thankful that over the years, God has placed mentors in my

---

[31] Barna, "New Research on the State of Discipleship," https://www.barna.com/research/new-research-on-the-state-of-discipleship/, December 1, 2015, accessed January 11, 2017.

life and has given me the great privilege of investing in scores of emerging leaders.[32] This chapter explores several qualities of a godly mentor.

Model Godly Behavior

The greatest gift you could give emerging leaders in the church, especially to those who may be called to ministry leadership, is to live a godly life before them. Peter told fellow elders and shepherds to be godly examples: *"Shepherd God's flock among you, not overseeing out of compulsion but willingly, as God would have you; not out of greed for money but eagerly; not lording it over those entrusted to you, but being examples to the flock. And when the chief Shepherd appears, you will receive the unfading crown of glory"* (1 Pet 5:2–4). Paul admonished the church at Philippi to follow his example: *"Do what you have learned and received and heard from me, and seen in me, and the God of peace will be with you"* (Phil 4:9).

You must begin by modeling a godly life before your disciples. They are looking for someone to give them direction and to model what a godly man or woman looks like in everyday life. They're looking for someone who can flesh out the faith by applying scriptural principles to real-life situations. This is especially true when things are not going well. How we react in times of crisis and in difficult situations reveals our true character. Do you respond by getting anxious and falling apart, or do you respond by trusting and depending on God?

Many years ago, I was helping lead a college trip across Texas to Mexico when our van broke down. Because it was a holiday weekend, we had a small window of time to act in securing transportation for part of our group. Rather than falling apart and thinking the trip was over, our student leaders turned to the group and asked them to pray. That's where we began, before anything else. We prayed for safety and guidance, but we also prayed that, whatever happened, God would be glorified. Soon, we secured a rental van and were on our way, but what I learned from that trip was the importance of rooting ourselves in prayer. Our leaders modeled what trusting God in the midst of a difficult situation looked like and taught our students more in their godly response than we could have taught them in a year of Bible studies.

---

[32] *The Merriam-Webster Dictionary*, online, s.v. "mentor."

Encourage and Affirm

Be a cheerleader to those you mentor. We have more than enough naysayers and critics in our lives, so be someone who encourages and affirms!

Intentionally affirm the good in your mentees' lives. Acknowledge and affirm godly character, attitudes, and actions. Look for ways to build them up and not tear them down. The author of Hebrews said, "And let us consider one another in order to provoke love and good works, not neglecting to gather together, as some are in the habit of doing, but encouraging each other, and all the more as you see the day approaching" (Heb 10:24–25). The following are some practical action steps you can take to encourage and affirm.

Applaud Even the Little Steps of Growth

Begin to speak into the lives of those you mentor, applauding even the smallest steps of growth you see displayed in their lives. Look for progress, and take the time to say something affirming for their good work, ideas, or meeting of specific goals and objectives. If language changes cultures and words impact worlds, then words of encouragement and affirmation can help move someone from good to great!

Be Supportive and Optimistic

Let your disciples or mentees know that you are on their team, that you love and support them, and that you want them to grow and succeed. Never get tired of telling them that you believe in them and their calling.

Help them to understand that God does not call the equipped; he equips the called. If God has called them to be leaders, he will give them all the resources needed to accomplish what he's called them to do. That includes helping them grow and develop as they depend upon him.

Chip came to faith as an older teenager. He participated in our collegiate ministry while he was still in high school. Although Chip's relationship with Christ was rich and growing, he came from a broken home and struggled with a lack of confidence. As we walked together, I began to help him understand that he was "accepted in the beloved" through Christ and that he has an amazing identity in Him. As the years went by, Chip grew to be a strong believer and disciple maker, investing in and mentoring many emerging leaders. Chip has a growing business in south Louisiana and is a bi-vocational pastor who is leading his church to make disciples who make disciples.

Never Cease Praying

When you pray for those you disciple and mentor, you are trusting God for a couple of things. First, when you pray you are trusting God to do what only he can do. As Paul said in 1 Corinthians 3:6–7, "I planted, Apollos watered, but God gave the growth. So, then, neither the one who plants nor the one who waters is anything, but only God who gives the growth." When you pray, you are believing that only God can grow a disciple of Christ.

Second, when you pray you are trusting God to help your disciple or mentee pursue Him. If the late Jerry Bridges was correct in saying, "Sanctification is a work that God does that requires our effort,"[33] then it stands to reason that you should pray that your disciple or mentee should have a heart to pursue God. You should pray often that God will awaken godly affections and a desire to know Christ in a deep, intimate way.

Pray and model prayer often with your disciples. Since prayer is caught as much as it is taught, you should pray often with your disciples or mentees. Show them that you are dependent on God and not yourself, and help them learn that prayer is a never-ending conversation with God. The Lord Jesus and the apostle Paul modeled prayer for their disciples. You should do the same!

Take Advantage of Teachable Moments

Most of the time, the thing that separates great mentors from mediocre ones is that great mentors take the initiative of walking through the open doors of opportunity. See those teachable moments, and take the initiative to share a word fitly spoken.

---

[33] Jerry Bridges, *Transforming Grace* (Colorado Springs: Tyndale Publishing House, 1991), 25.

Spend Time with Your Disciples

You will never earn the right or have the opportunity to share a timely word with your disciples or mentees unless you spend time with them. Notice what Paul said in 1 Thessalonians 2:8: "We cared so much for you that we were pleased to share with you not only the gospel of God but also our own lives because you had become dear to us."

When you share your life with others, it will cost you. You will have to set aside your own agenda and live intentionally for your mentee. As Paul wrote to the church at Philippi, "Do nothing out of selfish ambition or conceit, but in humility consider others as more important than yourselves. Everyone should look not to his own interests, but rather to the interests of others" (Phil 2:3–4).

Look for Teachable Moments

When you spend quality time with your mentees or disciples, look for teachable moments where God can use you to share a principle or truth when they are able to receive it.

When your mentees ask a question looking for an easy answer, you can respond with, "That's a great question. What do you think?" It's okay to leave your mentees hanging for a time without being quick to answer, letting them struggle with a question or a paradox.

This was one of Jesuss' chief teaching methods. He would frequently answer a question with a question. Notice the interaction between Jesus and his disciples in Matthew 16.

> *When Jesus came to the region of Caesarea Philippi, he asked his disciples, "Who do people say that the Son of Man is?"*
> *They replied, "Some say John the Baptist; others, Elijah; still others, Jeremiah or one of the prophets."*
> *"But you," he asked them, "who do you say that I am?"*
> *Simon Peter answered, "You are the Messiah, the Son of the living God."*
> *Jesus responded, "Blessed are you, Simon son of Jonah, because flesh and blood did not reveal this to you, but my Father in heaven." (Matt 16:13–17)*

Jesus asked a question, and then his disciples thought about it before answering. But notice how Jesus responded to their answer with another more direct question in verse 15: "Who do you say that I am?" Jesus did not let them repeat whatever the crowds were saying; He was asking them what they believed.

Offer Godly Counsel and Accountability

You should strive to help your disciples or mentees see things from God's viewpoint and not a human perspective—to see things through the lens of the Word of God and not by the wisdom of the world.

When offering godly counsel, base your counsel on the Word of God. Help them see principles that apply in the gray areas that Scripture has not specifically addressed, including answers to questions like these:

- Whom should I marry?
- Is it wrong to smoke or drink?
- Should I move to this city or another?

In addition to helping them address gray areas, you should offer them accountability. You must hold those you disciple up to God's standard for their lives, and not to your own. We all need someone in our lives who loves us well. We need someone who will ask the tough questions to hold us accountable for growth and ministry development and performance. In a growing, healthy, gospel-centered relationship, this accountability should never be abused, yet the truth remains: "We can't expect what we don't inspect."

First, this kind of relationship must be kingdom focused. The goal is to reach God's goal for growth and ministry, not the mentor's or that of the disciple maker. Second, the relationship should be voluntary. It is based on freedom in Christ, not some legalistic rule. In this relationship, there is no room for control, manipulation, or coercion. Third, this relationship should be flexible. Any healthy relationship must grow over time. This relationship should not be rigid, but it should leave room for adjustment and change.

Be Ready to Ask Deep Questions

A godly mentor should ask deep questions: questions that require more than a simple yes or no answer. Ask questions that require thought and reflection. Skilled mentors tend to ask question after question to help those whom they disciple or mentor to arrive at the answer for themselves.

In addition to asking deep questions, skilled mentors listen well. They listen to what is said and what is not said. They "hear between the lines" so that their understanding is deepened and the mentoring relationship can grow.

Share Spiritual Insights

Godly mentors and disciplemakers not only model lives that are consistent with the gospel, but they also share spiritual principles and insights. They take advantage of those teachable moments we talked about, and they share their faith in a systematic way. These should include things like the following.

Relationship with God

Godly mentors should model a rich and growing relationship with the Father as well as share meaningful spiritual insights that will help their disciples grow in their walks with God. Share things like helpful spiritual disciplines, scriptural precepts, and principles for spiritual growth.

Don't be afraid to share spiritual markers and real-life situations about how God worked to grow you and help you become more dependent on Him.

Servant Leadership

Another thing you should share with your mentee is the idea of servant leadership. A call to ministry is a call to lead the way Jesus did, as a servant: "For even the Son of Man did not come to be served, but to serve, and to give his life as a ransom for many" (Mark 10:45).

Discovering Spiritual Gifts

Help your mentees discover and use their spiritual gifts, especially those motivational gifts that will fuel their ministries. You can help them discover their spiritual gifts by using a spiritual gifts inventory and observing them as they serve and minister. When you recognize a particular gifting, encourage and talk to them about it. Be careful to ask deep questions and listen to their responses. Help them celebrate as they sense what God is doing in their lives.

Practical Ministry Skill Development

Give those you disciple opportunities to do some things they can use as they mature and develop—things like preparing and delivering a sermon or devotion, making a hospital visit, or leading one of the ordinances by officiating the Lord's Supper or baptism. When doing this, follow the model Jesus used from Scriptures:

- Jesus did it, and the disciples watched.
- Jesus did it, and the disciples assisted.
- The disciples did it, and Jesus assisted.
- The disciples did it, and Jesus watched.

It is important to be the model you want your mentees to follow. They shouldn't just hear what to do but rather observe what to do by watching you. Imitation may be a high form of flattery, but it is also a crucial part of learning how to live a godly life.

Chapter 7

Make Your Investment Count

Tim LaFleur

We've said a number of things about why and how to mentor emerging leaders in your communities and congregations. But what kinds of men should we consider investing in?

As shepherds, we are obviously for the good of all whom we serve, but these smaller, more intentional relationships should be reserved for only a select group of people. This does not mean a nationality or class of person but rather a man who is full of faith. Let's discover what these men of faith look like.

Finding Faithful Men

One of my favorite chapters of the New Testament is the second chapter of 2 Timothy. In this chapter, the apostle Paul uses seven metaphors to describe what a faithful pastor or gospel worker looks like:

- A steward who entrusts the gospel to faithful men.
- A soldier who endures hardship and desires to please his commander.
- An athlete who trains and competes according to the rules.
- A farmer who works hard planting, watering, cultivating, and harvesting.
- An approved worker who labors over the Word of God, rightly dividing the truth.

- A vessel fit for the Master's use.
- A servant desiring to please his Lord.

While all of these pictures are what a faithful pastor ought to look like, I want to call your attention to the steward who entrusts the gospel to faithful men.

According to the apostle Paul, a faithful pastor is like a steward. A steward is one who manages the resources or the affairs of another. The steward of Christ will not manage material wealth but spiritual treasures. He will entrust the precious treasure of the gospel to the faithful men, as Paul instructed Timothy in 2 Timothy 2:1–2: "You, therefore, my son, be strong in the grace that is in Christ Jesus. What you have heard from me in the presence of many witnesses, commit to faithful men who will be able to teach others also."

In this passage, the apostle Paul is admonishing his son in the faith, Timothy, to "be strong by the grace that is in Christ Jesus." In other words, Timothy will need to rely on God's grace as he fulfills his ministry. He will need to rely on the grace and strength that God will supply as Timothy depends on Him.

In addition, Paul tells Timothy to entrust the gospel "to faithful men who will be able to teach others also." This was Paul's practice in the early church to raise up pastors and gospel workers: to disciple and mentor "others also." Paul is telling Timothy that one of the things a faithful pastor should do is identify and invest in emerging leaders who would become pastors or gospel workers in the churches.

Paul told Timothy to look for faithful men to invest in, or men of faith. As it turns out, FAITH is a helpful acronym for the type of person you should look for when developing the kinds of relationships in this book: they should be Faithful, Available, Intentional about spiritual growth, Teachable, and Hungry for God.

In his book *Leaders Who Last*, Dave Kraft explains that one of the most important things that a pastor or leader in the church should do is identify, equip, and empower emerging leaders. And at the same time, he is amazed that so few pastors and church leaders are doing it.[34] If we need to make our investment count, we must ask God to help us identify the right men that we can "walk with" to help them grow and develop as leaders.

---

[34] Dave Kraft, *Leaders Who Last* (Wheaton: Good News, 2010).

In the early 1980s, while in seminary, I had the great privilege of serving at a church in Kennedale, Texas, near Ft. Worth. I served as associate pastor of youth and discipleship. It was a great place to learn and grow by not only doing ministry but by putting into practice what I was learning in seminary. One of the highlights of my time of ministry there was the opportunity to learn from and to be mentored by the senior pastor, Earnest Wall. Brother Earnest had been called to ministry leadership later in life and had spent many years in the marketplace as a small business owner. I learned from Brother Wall how to see the potential in people—to see them not for who they are but for what they could become as they grow spiritually.

As we invest in emerging leaders, we must embrace that same mindset, seeing the potential in men as they grow in their faith and surrender to the lordship of Christ. Because we have a limited amount of time to invest in emerging leaders, we must select the right men to walk with. Before we select these men, we must spend time in prayer to discern God's will. In Luke 6, Scripture tells us that the Lord Jesus spent all night in prayer before selecting his apostles. If the Son of God spent all night in prayer before selecting twelve men he would invest in, so likewise we should pray for those we are discipling.

Let's see what it looks like to find men who are faithful, available, intentional about spiritual growth, teachable, and hungry for God.

Faithful

If we want our investment to count, we must mentor and disciple emerging leaders who have demonstrated faithfulness. By definition, someone who is faithful is committed to someone or something. Further, it's the idea of being loyal and following through with what you have committed to do. Faithful men not only talk a good game, but they demonstrate their faithfulness by their manner of life.

Several years ago, I had the privilege of serving a small church in south Louisiana. While serving there, I had the privilege of leading a young man named Mardy to faith in Christ. Mardy worked out in the oil field and was recovering from an injury requiring surgery. During his time of recovery, I had the opportunity to disciple him.

When we began to meet together in discipleship, I explained to Mardy that over the time of our meeting we would memorize twenty-six verses of Scripture. The next week, I called him to make sure we could meet at the appointed time. But before we hung up, Mardy told me that he memorized all twenty-six verses. I thought to myself, "You did not memorize all those verses in a week." So, I began to quiz him and sure enough, he not only memorized every verse, but he got them word-perfect. In the weeks ahead, Mardy demonstrated a faithfulness to God, to Scripture, to his family, and to serving at church. As Mardy and I walked together, it became obvious that God had a calling on his life.

During that season in my ministry, I had the opportunity to travel and preach all over south Louisiana, and Mardy would accompany me and share his testimony about the difference Jesus made in his life. Before long, Mardy began to work with the students at his church and then was called to pastor a church in south Louisiana. Twenty-five years later, Pastor Mardy Guidry is the pastor of the Fellowship Baptist Church in Denham Springs, Louisiana.

Available

When looking for the right kind of men to invest in, we have already seen that they must have demonstrated faithfulness. In addition, they must be available. In other words, they must have the time to be in a mentoring relationship. They can't be so committed to other endeavors that they don't have the necessary time to give themselves to something else on the calendar. God may be inviting them to become involved with Him and his work, but they are not available because they have already committed to other things.

When encountering these men, you must discern whether they truly have a desire to follow the call and work on next steps or if they are really not interested in pursuing God or his plans for them.

When I have discerned that a man truly has a desire to pursue God and his call on their lives, I have found it helpful to grab coffee or lunch and have an honest conversation with him. I try to encourage him to continue to "go hard after God" and to follow the leadership of the Holy Spirit in his life; but perhaps this is not the right season for us to walk together because he's got so much on his plate right now. Then I'll make a plan to circle back in two or three months to talk about it again.

Intentional

When I was a freshman at LSU, I was a member of a campus ministry called the Navigators. During the Fall of the year, I committed to be in a discipleship group that would meet every Monday afternoon. We would study the Bible, memorize Scripture, hold each other accountable, and pray for one another. As a new believer in Christ, walking with these guys was life giving!

Early on our D-Group's leader, Johnny (an upperclassman), challenged us with a quote by Dawson Trotman, the founder of the Navigators: "Only three things are eternal: God, his Word, and the souls of men. Invest in these things." If you want to make your investment count, find men who are intentional about the things of God, men who want to pursue God's calling on their lives and are intentional about being obedient to God as he reveals their next steps.

It is written in Proverbs, "The path of the righteous is like the light of dawn, shining brighter and brighter until midday" (Prov 4:18). What a wonderful promise! This verse promises that when we walk in the light that we have, God will give more light. In other words, when we obey God in the things he has clearly revealed to us, he will be faithful to reveal more of his will to us.

Lord, lead us to invest in those men who are available to give themselves to walking with us and intentional about pursuing the call You have on their lives!

Teachable

Several years ago during a Q & A panel, Someone asked me, "What kind of men will you not disciple? I responded by saying, "I can walk with almost anyone, but I guess the deal breaker for me is someone who is not teachable."

Being teachable by definition is the ability to learn or to be taught. When I talk about someone who is teachable, I am not talking about someone who has the *ability* to be taught as much as someone who has the *desire* to be taught. I want to invest in men who have a desire to learn. You should mentor men who have not only a general desire to learn but a specific desire to learn from you and others in your group.

When I pastored my first church, I was blessed to walk with several young men who sensed God had a calling on their lives. Every Thursday afternoon we would meet for discipleship and practical ministry together. It was a kind of life-on-life discipleship, and for the practical ministry skills we used Jesus's model of discipleship as outlined in the previous chapter.

During our time together, these young men (who were teenagers) memorized Scripture, learned how to do inductive Bible study, discussed theology, and read books together. They learned how to share their faith using a New Testament, a gospel tract, and how to share their testimony. In addition, they learned and practiced practical ministry skills such as home and hospital visitation, organizing and leading a small group, and serving as decision-time counselors at youth rallies.

Today four of those young men (not so young anymore) serve in full-time gospel ministry. One is a seminary professor and three are pastors. One of the pastors earned a PhD in expository preaching. One thing that they all have in common is a desire to learn! I love the Scripture: "Instruct the wise, and he will be wiser still; teach the righteous, and he will learn more" (Prov 9:9). If you want to make your investment count, find men who have a desire to learn and be taught.

Hungry for God

Jesus said in the beatitudes, "Blessed are those who hunger and thirst for righteousness, for they shall be filled" (Matt 5:6). What a promise! Those who hunger and thirst for righteousness will be filled and satisfied. You can be assured that when you mentor and disciple men who are hungry and thirsty for the things of God that they will be "all in."

This "heart hunger" is also described in the Psalms: "God, you are my God; I eagerly seek you. I thirst for you; my body faints for you in a land that is dry, desolate, and without water. So I gaze on you in the sanctuary to see your strength and your glory" (Ps 63:1–2). In this text, the psalmist has a hunger that only God can satisfy! He likened his desire for God and his presence as one who is dying of thirst in a desert. He longs for God and the presence of God!

Several years ago, while pastoring a small church in south Louisiana, I had the privilege of mentoring a young man named Jessie. Only a teenager, Jessie had a real hunger for God and the things of God. He loved to be in God's presence, to worship, and to study his Word. He saw God as his treasure and desired a deep intimate relationship with him.

I remember stopping by his house one day to speak to him, but he was not home. His mother told me that he had taken his Bible and his cassette player and went to a place in the field behind his house to be alone with God. I walked over to the place where his mother said he would be and found him under a shade tree on a blanket listening to praise music reading his Bible. The point is this: Jessie had a heart hunger for God. Jesus was his treasure, and because he had a hunger and thirst for God, he spent time with Him. He loved to be in his presence.

The men you mentor and disciple don't have to have all of the qualities that we talked about but they should have some of them. Look for men of FAITH!

Chapter 8

Intentionally Calling the Younger Generations

Rob Millman

The summer is an amazing season, a vibrant time of celebration as churches throughout the country reach out to the younger generations. We have two primary generations of focus, Generation Z, comprised of young people born between 1997 and 2012, currently ranging from thirteen to twenty-six years of age; and Generation Alpha, those born after 2013 and currently comprising children in kindergarten to upcoming sixth graders of this approaching school year. According to some experts, the most impressionable years are between twelve and twenty-four years of age. It is extremely important during these impressionable years to share Christ with young people. A study completed by Barna reports children ages 5–13 have a 32 percent probability of accepting Christ, youth ages 14–18 have only have a 14 percent probability of doing so, and unbelieving adults over the age of 19 only a 6 percent probability of becoming Christians.

The first call is always the call to salvation, and it is imperative that all Christians understand the immediacy of importance to reach the younger generations. The second call is the call to spiritual growth and discipleship, which is important especially for the Gen Z generation who have accepted Christ. It is essential for those in this age group to be engaged in connecting with peers, as their influence may provide a strong persuasion to consider dialing-in on their spiritual growth. The practice of the spiritual disciplines in this age group is important, including meeting to study the Word, memorizing and sharing Scripture, worshiping through praise, and also engaging in community outreach to serve others. The third call is the call to ministry leadership. Dr. Howard Culbertson, a professor at the Southern Nazarene University shared, "Many people serving as career cross-cultural missionaries have testified that they first felt God calling them to missionary service during that 4–14 age period."[35]

Looking back on history of those called at a young age, there are many names that come to mind. From the 1700s there is George Whitefield, who undoubtably felt the call to preach as a young man and was ordained while pursuing his bachelor's degree. In the 1800s the prince of preachers Charles Spurgeon was called to preach as teenager. Spurgeon at age fifteen came to faith in January, was baptized in April, and within a year of accepting Christ began preaching. In the 1900s Billy Graham accepted Christ at age sixteen; after graduating high school he attended a school whose rules and coursework he felt were too legalistic and was nearly expelled. He transferred to Florida Bible Institute and in 1937 started preaching. Adrian Rogers served at Bellevue Baptist Church in Memphis, Tennessee, for thirty-three years. He felt called to preach at a young age and entered ministry at nineteen years of age. H. B. Charles was baptized at the age of six and preached his first message at the tender age of eleven years old under the watchful eyes of his father and other pastoral leaders in the congregation at Mount Sinai Missionary Baptist Church in Los Angeles, California. His father passed away, and H. B., at the age of seventeen, proceeded his father as the pastor of the church. These stories may seem dramatic; however, these men felt a sense of God calling at a young age. It is not inconceivable that young men today in the twenty-first century would also feel the call of God upon their lives.

We want to implore ministry leaders and especially pastors to take note of young people in your midst who are seeking God. Jesus selected young men to follow him as his disciples. It is noted in the context of first-century Jewish tradition, a child began his religious training at age five and would continue until twelve or thirteen years of age. A young man who considered rabbi training would begin at thirteen to fifteen years of age, and at age thirty he could have disciples of his own. Jesus used ordinary men, Andrew was considered to be a little older than Jesus, and Peter was married; however, John was considered to the youngest, most likely a

---

[35] Howard Culbertson, "At what age do Americans become Christian," https://home.snu.edu/~hculbert/ages.htm, accessed March 21st, 2025.

teenager. Based upon statistics and the few examples of life stories shared, it is essential to intentionally reach young people.

In summary, there are many young people who need to hear the gospel message, and maybe the voice that makes a difference in a life and death decision with eternal impact is from the young person in your church. The facts bear truth that proactive ministry in the younger generations is imperative and requires an active, hands-on approach by pastors to recognize the impact of Christ on young lives and how their impressions will affect future generations.

Section 4

Ministry Toolbox

The definition of a tool is "a device or implement, especially held in one hand, used to carry out a specific function."[36]

Most toolboxes you carry around with you have two sections; after you open the lid there is a tray with a handle with easy-to-grab tools you would use regularly like pliers or a screwdriver. The bigger tools, like bigger wrenches and hammers, are found in the larger compartment. In this toolbox, similarly, we have included some tools we feel will be of real value to those aspiring to be engaged in ministry leadership and also for pastors and ministry leaders to "call out the called."

---

[36] *The Merriam-Webster Dictionary*, online, s.v. "tool."

You will find in the first section of this toolbox call-to-ministry testimonies, which we feel are invaluable to aid men considering the call to ministry to witness first-hand how God calls.

In the second section of this toolbox you will find two call-to-ministry sermons. Our hope is these messages provide inspiration for pastors to intentionally "call out the called" on a more ongoing basis. We want these sample messages to be a catalyst to encourage pastors to increase the frequency with which they encourage their flocks to evaluate how God wants to use men and women for his purpose.

In the third section, you will discover the proven methods Tim LaFleur used for years to mentor emerging leaders in a group dynamic. Tim has provided an outline to mentor men in a small-group setting. Tim's work as a Baptist campus minister at Nicholls State University, combined with local-church experience in both normative and megachurch environments, has yielded a great crop of ministry leaders. He has over one hundred men and women as part of his ministry tree. Both the local pastor and association leader will find this information to be of great value to mentor men in a group setting.

Finally, we have also included a list of additional reading resources related to the call of ministry.

Chapter 9

Call-to-Ministry Testimonies

One of the best ways to determine how God calls is to study the lives of others who have been called. We want to encourage you if you are aspiring to be involved in ministry leadership to ask your pastor about his call to ministry. We believe you will find reading and listening to call-to-ministry testimonies provides special insight to discover how the Lord leads men on a path for service. We also suggest you visit FollowtheCall.org and listen to the testimonies of pastors there.

In preparing this book as a resource to you, we asked the men who serve on the Follow the Call Ministries Advisory Council to each share their call to ministry testimonies. In the next few pages, you will find their testimonies written in first person and provided for your encouragement.

Bob Burton's Call to Ministry

"I ran from God like Jonah." It seemed to me every pastor had this kind of call story. I thought this was normal as I heard preachers repeat these words of struggle. Well, this was not my testimony, and mine was quite the opposite. Let me highlight three spiritual influences God used in my life (they don't include a whale).

A Devotion to Jesus

The calling came through a deepening devotion to my Savior. At age seventeen, the Father opened my eyes to the truth that there is no greater love than for one to lay down his life for his friends (John 15:13). I became a Christian with a newborn desire to love Him with all my heart, my soul, my mind, and my strength. This meant my "Yes" was on the table for anything he had in mind because he first loved me.

A Work of the Word of God

I had an ever-growing appetite for the Bible. I had an interest in a career related to aviation; yet God had another thing in mind. I said to Him, "Everyone says they fought the call but, this is something I would really desire to do for You." Then I read in 1 Timothy 3:1, "If a man desires to be a pastor, it's a good thing." There were many more of these instances, but God always had an answer in his Word.

A Supportive Church Family

This call did not all happen in a vacuum, because I was a part of a loving church family. The pastor as well as others affirmed my gifts and calling. They discipled me, gave me opportunities to serve, and extended grace. There is a blessing beyond measure to know God has called you and to run towards that call. Thanks be to God!

About Bob Burton

He serves as Association Mission Strategist for the Salem South Baptist Association in Illinois. He formerly served as the Midwest Regional Equipper for the SEND Network. Bob is a former pastor and graduated with his MDiv. from Midwestern Baptist Seminary and received his doctorate from The Southern Baptist Theological Seminary in Christian education and leadership.

Clint Calvert's Call to Ministry

"The boundary lines have fallen for me in pleasant places; indeed, I have a beautiful inheritance." (Psalm 16:6)

My first pleasant place was a family who worked hard and followed Christ. I was born in Texas and reared in a Christian home. My father owned and operated a few different small businesses. I went to work beside my father at an early age. My mother was active in church and brought me along. I accepted Christ as my Lord and Savior as a child growing up in an Independent Missionary Baptist church. The dual influence of my father George's work ethic and my mother Mary's reverence for God shaped me to be a person who would have one foot in the marketplace and one foot in the ministry.

My second pleasant place was Terrell Christian Academy. In my early teen years, my mother took me and my siblings to a Southern Baptist church in our hometown. Our church youth group participated in short-term mission trips to Minnesota. On one of these trips in 1984, I sensed that God was calling me to tell others about Jesus and to use my influence in a positive way. Church leaders helped me to discern this call as a call to ministry leadership. Our church also sponsored a Christian school, Terrell Christian Academy, where I was surrounded by teachers and peers who were following Jesus. I was one of five students in the school who heard God's call to ministry and my pastor, Mike Smith, mentored all five of us, giving teenage boys opportunities to preach, lead worship, visit nursing homes, and serve in volunteer roles.

My third pleasant place was at the feet of mentors who loved me, challenged me, and gave me ministry opportunities. My pastor Mike Smith's mentorship persisted from my teen years and well into my middle age. I have also been mentored by Chip Ingram, Jim Leach, James Shields, Donnie Auvenshine, Charlie McLaughlin, John Burke, Jack Bell, Charles Harvey, Scott Speight, and Leo Endel. I have been so blessed by mentors, and now it is my turn to provide mentorship to others.

My fourth pleasant place is Rochester, Minnesota, with my role as Church Leadership Catalyst of the Minnesota-Wisconsin Baptist Convention. Little did I know as a teenage Texan, called to ministry in Minnesota, that I would get to move to Minnesota in 1998 and serve for most of my ministry. Beginning in 2006, God gave me opportunities with Midwestern Baptist Theological Seminary and later Southeastern Baptist Theological Seminary to provide ministry training to Minnesota and Wisconsin church leaders on undergraduate, graduate, and doctoral levels. I have also been trained by Clinical Pastoral Education International to facilitate clinical pastoral education (CPE). CPE increases the self-awareness, ministry skills, and economic opportunities of church leaders in the two states I serve. Most of my students are mid-career adults who are responding to God's call to ministry leadership after having a career in the marketplace.

Not everyone has all the blessings I have been given. As the Psalmist wrote in PS 16:6 "The boundary lines have fallen to me in pleasant places; indeed, I have a delightful inheritance." I live out my calling knowing God provided for the influence to shape me. These gifts must be shared to provide leadership development for others. I serve from an embarrassment of riches that God has lavishly supplied to equip me to encourage others for readiness in ministry. God gave me a Christian family, a church-based education, many mentors, and opportunities to serve. This is my delightful inheritance.

About Clint Calvert

He serves as the Leadership Catalyst for the Minnesota-Wisconsin Baptist Convention and as an adjunct professor for Southeastern Seminary. He received his M.A. at Southwestern and doctorate from Gateway Seminary

David Wheeler's Call to Ministry Testimony

I grew up in a small neighborhood outside of Nashville, Tennessee. My parents were both committed Christians. I can remember our house being the one place in our neighborhood where everyone was always welcome.

My earliest memories of my mom were going with her to deliver meals to hurting and sick neighbors. The same was true with my dad. I recall one Christmas Eve as a seven year old when we delivered toys to a family in our neighborhood. Somehow, my dad found out that the father had abandoned the family earlier in December, leaving the mother to choose between feeding her three kids or providing Christmas presents. Even though my mom was recovering from a near-fatal kidney condition, leaving huge medical bills, my dad was determined to help. He explained, "There is no way I could sleep knowing those three children would not have a Christmas."

Many of my unsaved friends stayed at our house on numerous occasions. This was especially helpful to open doors for spiritual conversations. In time, some of those friends were saved. Those moments had a huge impact on my early life.

When I was ten years old, I recall having a conversation with my mom and grandmother. I can remember this moment like it was yesterday. They asked me what I was going to do when I grew up. Without even pondering the thought, for the first time in my life I said, "I am going to be a preacher." As you can imagine, saying that made both my mom and grandmother exceptionally happy.

In the years to come, when I was involved in things that did not glorify God, my mom and grandmother never ceased to pray for me. I am convinced, without their prayers, I may have ended up in a totally different situation in my life and vocation.

When I was sixteen, I started to question my faith and for the first time began to consider my calling. The initial step occurred when I went before my church one Sunday evening to personally address numerous hypocrisies related to my faith. As a result, I recommitted my life to Christ and was rebaptized. I was tired of being miserable; my desire was to go all in and embrace my faith once and for all!

It was during this time that I was challenged to share my faith for the first time. My youth pastor gave me an outline for the Romans Road with the instructions to share the gospel with at least one unsaved person that week. Fast forward to Tuesday evening. I invited a girl to come over to my house, and much to my surprise, she accepted my offer! Somehow, we ended up outside shooting basketball. About ten minutes into our shoot-around, God began to whisper in my ear something like, "David, you remember that Romans Road outline you received Sunday night, this is a perfect time to share it with this young lady."

Just being real, I was totally petrified! But after several uncomfortable minutes, I asked her if she went to church. Much to my chagrin, she told me "No." Next up, I asked if she was a Christian, and again she said something like, "not that I can recall." Ultimately, after asking these questions, I finally listened to the Holy Spirit and invited her inside my house to share the Romans Road outline. To say the least, the presentation lacked continuity and confidence. I was surprised that my presentation didn't drive her away from both me and Jesus!

Eventually I asked her if she understood what I shared. To my surprise, she acknowledged that she was a sinner and expressed her need to be forgiven! Despite my obvious fears and shortcomings, the Holy Spirit won out! Believe it or not, she was saved that night, and I have never got over it! As a side note, I married that girl seven years later.

Something happened in me as I saw God working through his glorious gospel. That evening changed the direction of my life. For the first time, I started reconnecting with the calling I felt as a ten-year-old child. A few years later, after being mentored by numerous people, at the age of twenty I finally walked up in front of my church and publicly embraced

God's call as a pastor, teacher, and evangelist. There was instant peace, joy, and a deep sense of excitement.

Over forty years later, there still is!

About David Wheeler

He serves as a professor of evangelism at Liberty University. David is a former pastor and served as Evangelism and Prayer Director for the Indiana Baptist Convention. He received his MDiv. and PhD. from Southwestern Baptist Seminary.

Jonathan LaFleur's Call to Ministry

I have loved God's Word since I was child. At the age of twelve I began attending a Christian school that required I get a new Bible—the one I had at that time was a picture Bible for kids. So, my mom took me to the Good News Bookstore in Houma, Louisiana, to buy my first "grown-up Bible." It was blue and silver, the colors of my new school, and had my name inscribed right on the front cover. I swelled with pride and excitement when I held it for the first time and flipped through its pages.

I went home that night and opened my new Bible right down the middle and began reading Psalm 1. Then I read Psalm 2, Psalm 3, and so on until, way past my bedtime, I had finished reading the entire book of Psalms. Time seemed to be irrelevant—I was completely consumed in the Scriptures. In that moment I knew two things: I loved the Bible, and I wanted to help others love it as much as I do.

Two years later I began attending Wednesday night youth group with my friend Clay at his church. They had a new youth minister named Eric who was fresh out of seminary and passionate about discipleship. One night at youth group, for no apparent reason at all, Eric pointed at Clay and me and said, "You two guys are going to start leading our youth group in musical worship."

We looked around wondering if he was actually speaking to us or someone else. We realized he was indeed talking to us and questioned whether he was being serious or joking. We had no leadership experience or musical talent at the time, but Eric saw the potential in us and was used by God to draw it out. We did begin leading worship for the youth group; we did so for the next five years and eventually became quite good.

About the same time we started leading worship, Eric began discipling us, pouring into us all that he knew about living for the Lord. He studied the Bible with us, challenged us, befriended us, and gave us more and more opportunities to serve in the youth group and the church. During one of our many discipleship group meetings, I finally shared with Eric what I had been feeling for years by this point, that the Lord was calling me to ministry leadership.

When I told Eric this, he promptly responded, "I have no doubt that is true. In fact, I have seen it in you since the time I picked you out to lead worship for our youth group." Then he prayed for me, specifically that I would not neglect the Word of God, the gift he has given me, or the call to preach his name. And to this day, over twenty years later, I can say to God's glory and only by his grace, I have not neglected to follow the call.

About Jonathan LeFleur

He serves as the Lead Pastor at First Southern Baptist Church in Terre Haute, Indiana. Jonathan has pastored there since July 2017. He received his MDiv. from New Orleans Baptist Seminary.

Julio Varela's Call to Ministry

Julio was born in Torreon Coahuila, Mexico in a Catholic family on August 20, 1973. He is the oldest of four boys. In God's faithfulness and mercy, his grandmother became a Christian and invited Julio's mother to come to the church. Julio and his mother started going to church when Julio was just five years old. Julio received the Lord as his personal savior at the age of thirteen and was baptized. He consecrated his life to the Lord when he was seventeen years old. At the age of eighteen he attended a missions' conference and knew he needed to serve God full time. However, following his father's advice he went to college and got a degree in computer science. Julio served in his local church all that time as a youth leader and part of the preaching team. After finishing college, he found a job and worked for four years for a company in San Luis Potosi, where he met Alma and married her on December 20, 1997. Together they served the Lord in different capacities in their home church in San Luis Potosi, Mexico.

One of these roles was the role of a youth pastor. As a youth pastor Julio took the youth to several recreational and spiritual activities. One of those activities was a missions' conference where Julio and his wife Alma thought and hoped the Lord would call some of the youth to ministry. Unexpectedly, the Lord call Julio and Alma to ministry. After the conferences they talked to the speaker and got some advice on how to start the process. One essential recommendation was to find a place to get equipped for ministry. Julio's passion for the Word of God moved him to look for a place in which he could learn Greek and Hebrew.

Julio and Alma, obeying God's voice, quit their jobs and left their country, family, and friends to come to the Rio Grande Bible College, in Edinburg, Texas, to prepare to serve the Lord full time. While still studying in RGBI God called them to serve Him there. So, in July 2003 they went to Calvary Bible College and Theological Seminary in Kansas City, Missouri, where Julio got his master's degrees in theology, Bible, and divinities. Julio and Alma came back to RGBI in May 2007 and served the Lord as professors in the Bible Institute and the language school. During this time Julio also finished his PhD in theology.

Julio and Alma left Rio Grande in 2019 and went to Colorado. Julio was invited to be part of the pastoral team of a supporting church in Colorado Springs. However, the Lord brought them back to Edinburg, Texas, the same year. It was hard leaving the church in Colorado, but it was better to be obedient to God than staying there. Julio started as an interim pastor for the Spanish service in his previous church in January 2020. Then, in May of 2021 Dr. Larry Windle contacted Julio and extended the invitation to come back as the vice president of education. Julio accepted in May 2021 and was ministering there until the Lord called him to come to San Antonio, Texas, to serve as the academic dean at the Baptist University of the Américas. Alma and Julio started a journey that changed their lives when they were obedient and started following the call that Lord gave them, and they can both say it's been a blessing and an honor.

About Julio Varela

Juilo serves as Pastor of United Baptist Church in Laredo, Texas. He previously served as academic dean at the Baptist University of the Americas, and his previous role was as vice president of education at the Rio Grande Bible Institute. He received his MDiv. from Calvary University and his PhD at Piedmont International University.

Kurt Owens's Call to Ministry

There was a time my picture could have been posted next to the term "Antichrist" in the dictionary. It was not so much the idea that I was an unbeliever as it was that my lifestyle screamed antichrist. Ironically, I grew up a preacher's kid and spent most of my childhood attempting to prove that only my parents were saved. I was driven by a need for acceptance and validation. Though I sought acceptance, I experienced years of rejection from the in-crowd. I lacked a great deal of self-esteem and internalized myself as an outsider. Even at church I did not measure up to the rest of the people. I felt as though I did not belong there. In spite of being a PK, I felt as if I was doomed to hell. I never understood why I had to beg God to save and accept me, so I eventually gave up on trying to please him.

Instead, I turned to the streets of Milwaukee. After becoming a successful drug dealer, my peers more than accepted me. As a dope dealer, I wore the best clothing, drove the best cars, and had plenty of beautiful women. I made a ton of money and simply purchased acceptance and validation from others. Nevertheless, my lavish lifestyle also made me a target. I was robbed three separate times. Astonishingly, it was not until the last robbery at gunpoint that I seriously began considering life after death. I will never forget that day when two guns were pointed at my head.

As the gunmen ordered me to kneel down, it appeared as if I only had enough time left to ask God to forgive me. Surprised that I was still alive, I followed up my request for forgiveness with a promise. I promised God if he could get me out of that particular situation, I would change my life for the better. In a strange twist of fate, the gunmen did not pull the trigger and instead demanded I lead them to the money. Though they had already robbed me for the drugs, they wanted more. Be that as it may, I led them to the top porch on the second floor of my home and reached underneath the banister as though I had money hidden there. All in one swoop, I did a complete 360 and flipped my body off the porch while landing on my shoeless feet. While there is no reasonable explanation of how that was possible, God not only heard me but spared my life that day. I was forever changed!

From that day forward I began a nonstop examination of what would have happened to my soul if I had been killed that day. Though I knew I needed Christ in my life, I also knew I did not measure up to the Christians in my dad's church. I was clueless on how to live a holy, righteous life.

However, I did keep my vow to the Lord. I completely turned away from my life as a drug dealer and took a job working as a delivery driver for a pharmaceutical company. How ironic is that?

My boss took a keen interest in me and began to pour into my life. He told me he wanted to teach me the business, brought me into the warehouse, and from there, into the front office. He trained me on everything there was in the company, and by the time the year was up I had worked my way up to the top of that branch. A couple of months later, I was promoted to our corporate office in Jackson, Mississippi. In a period of eighteen months, I had gone from being a street thug dope dealer to running thirteen branches nationwide. By this time, I knew without a shadow of a doubt that God was at work in my life.

A couple of weeks after arriving in Jackson, an older white gentleman knocked at my door. He said he was in the neighborhood and simply wanted to share the good news of the gospel. I responded by telling him he would only be wasting his time because I was a pastor's kid and I already knew about the gospel. Thankfully, he did not accept my response. I remember him asking me, "If you were to die tonight and sat at God's door, what would you say to him in an effort to get in?" I said something along the lines of my good outweighing my bad. It was then he informed me salvation had nothing to do with what I had done in life. However, his statement went against everything I had ever believed about salvation.

He then shared a passage of Scripture with me I had never seen before. It was Romans 10:9 and said, "If you declare with your mouth, 'Jesus is Lord,' and believe in your heart that God raised him from the dead, you will be saved." I argued back and forth with the man about my need to be holy and perfect, but he kept pointing to the Scripture. All my life I believed I had to get right before being accepted as a Christian. That night I tossed and turned, wondering how that Scripture could be true in spite of my imperfections. I cried like a baby when it finally hit me. I thought to myself, if this Scripture is true, I received salvation at the age of nine. That night, still imperfect and unrighteous, I came into the knowledge of my salvation. For the first time in life, I knew I had been covered and accepted through Christ's love.

Since that night, I have had such great peace and tranquility knowing that Christ has secured eternal life on my behalf. I will never forget the near-death experience nor the night I came into the knowledge of my salvation. Those two days have impacted me forever. The biggest change I have noticed in my life after receiving Christ is the fact I no longer seek validation or acceptance from others. All of my emotional and spiritual needs are filled through the love of Christ. I came to realize he is all I need. Today, I am much more merciful, forgiving, patient, and loving to other imperfect people because I am forever reminded of the same being granted to me.

About Kurt Owens

He serves as the Lead Pastor of UFlourish Church in Milwaukee, Wisconsin. Kurt is the founder of Bridge Builders, inspiring inner-city innovation. He received his M.A. in Christian ministry from Liberty University and Ed.D. in organizational leadership and Christian education from Grand Canyon University.

Warren Gasaway's Call to Ministry

God's call to ministry often looks very different for most. At the age of twenty-four, while serving as a department head of creative services for a television station, my wife, two-year-old son, and I knelt down in our little apartment and finally surrendered to ministry. Our simple prayer was, "Wherever, whenever, whatever you want us to do." We knew that those words and the heart behind them could take us in a very different direction. However, we had no idea of the now twenty-five-year adventure he had for us.

My background didn't necessarily shape us for ministry. I didn't grow up in a devoutly religious family. Having gone to a large, secular university, I didn't have any Bible college or seminary. I didn't have much experience in church leadership. However, after God's leading through certain passages of Scripture (especially 1 Timothy), over a year of prayer and fasting, encouragement from leaders, and passion for reaching people, Melissa and I were firmly convinced that he was calling us to a life of full-time service to him. While struggling with this call, a few close friends gave opportunities for experience to discover if God was truly working that call out in our lives.

Not knowing where such a surrender would lead, we were simply resolved to follow the next step he provided, whether that be seminary, the mission field, or bi-vocational work. Three months after surrendering a church asked me to speak at a youth retreat. I didn't know they were looking for a youth minister, nor did I know that most of the search team would be there. After the service, they asked for a resume. I thought they were just being kind. Two months later, I was going in view of a call to a place I would serve for over eleven years. God confirmed the call on our lives. During my time there, the church supported furthering my seminary education and gave multiple experiences for leadership, preaching, and shepherding people.

The call to ministry is his call and is his work for his glory, so he is the one who works in us to equip. I believe that God's will for our lives can be found in surrender. He shows us his will through possibilities, through prayer, through our God-given passions, through encouragement from people, through peace in surrender, and through passages of Scripture. God's call may look different person to person, but he uses some of the same nudges to show people what he is doing. And he's always at work growing us for the assignments he gives.

Since God's call on our lives, I have served as a youth and children minister, an associate pastor, a family pastor, a youth strategist on convention staff, an assistant team leader, and now a team leader for a convention. God has called me into many interim pastor roles, to lead statewide ministry efforts, and to give direction for partnering hundreds of churches. None of these roles nor ministries were on my mind when God called. We couldn't have conceived such works. Only he could ever lead and provide for his plans. All we wanted was to serve "wherever, whenever, whatever."

My prayer is for a next generation of leaders recognizing the great call of God to lead and shepherd people to love Him and others. Surrendering to his will in that call continues to be the great joy of our lives.

About Warren Gasaway

He serves as the director of evangelism and collegiate student ministry specialist for the Arkansas Baptist State Convention. He received his MDiv. from Southwestern Baptist Theological Seminary.

Mark Millman's Call to Ministry

My call to ministry took place over a period of time. One concept I struggled with is that I really believe a call to salvation is a call to ministry for all believers. Some of us are called to be equippers. So, this testimony is how I was called into leadership as an equipper.

The spring of 1989 was when I can remember as the pivotal time for me. After looking for a job for almost two years after graduating from college, I had two job offers. One was to be a computer programmer with Electronic Data Systems. The second option was to be a two-year missionary in church planting with the Home Mission Board of the Southern Baptist Convention.

After much prayer and struggling for several weeks that turned into months, God led me to take the position in Orlando that started in August of 1989. I passed up a lot more money, benefits, and a "softer" life. Many around me did not think I was making the right decision.

But through God's Word, prayer, and the encouragement of key people, I moved to Orlando with the help of my parents in August of 1989. For the next two years my supervisor would pray with me monthly what my next steps would be. I served church plants across central Florida in many different ways.

During that time God was able to show Himself to me. As my time was ending in Orlando in 1991, I made the decision to attend Golden Gate Baptist Theological Seminary in Mill Valley, California. My seminary experience also proved to be life transformation with the relationships I developed along with my studies.

As I look back, I know that God used this period of time to call me into ministry leadership as an equipper and leader of people. Although I am far from perfect, I can look back now to see how God used this time to shape and mold me with his hand on my life.

About Mark Millman

He serves as the North American Mission Board church planting catalyst for the State of Wisconsin. Previously, Mark served in churches in Florida and New Jersey. He received his undergraduate in business administration from Indiana State University. He received his MDiv. and DMin in evangelism, missions, and church growth from the Southern Baptist Theological Seminary.

Chapter 10
Call-to-Ministry Sermons

In this section we have provided two "call to ministry" sermons, the first is based on Romans 10:14–15 and the second on 2 Timothy 2:1–2. The messages are formatted in a style developed by Dr. Wayne McDill, former professor of preaching at Southeastern Baptist Theological Seminary. Rob prepared these messages as a tool for you, the reader. We felt one of the reasons for the gap in today's ministry pipeline is not enough pastors are preaching messages to "call out the called." Hence the purpose of providing these samples is to be of encouragement and truly embolden pastors to preach messages similar to these. Our hope is you will find these to be of value.

Romans 10:14–15 Call-to-Ministry Message

Introduction

In the mid-nineteenth century in large cities, newspaper publishers would have young newspaper boys sell newspapers on street corners to sell special editions. Often, to get the attention of the crowd, these boys would shout "Extra! Extra read all about it!" They did this to get those passing by on the sidewalks to buy a newspaper. Usually, these young boys would first shout the headline to trigger a response so people would buy the newspapers because they wanted to read more about the story behind the headline and get the facts. Today as twenty-first century Christians we have a story with an astounding headline and amazing facts. The question at hand: Who is shouting out to get the attention of a lost and broken world?

Prayer

So, let's begin our day with prayer:

Dear Heavenly Father,

This day we ask for your power to work through our lives to reach the world with the gospel message of salvation to take to every corner, every place, every cranny throughout this world. Let us be able to touch those who seem untouchable, take away our fears, strengthen us with faith, courage and zeal to boldly proclaim to the world that Jesus Christ is Lord. And for those with us here today that truly do not know you, we pray you open their eyes and open their hearts to the love of our Savior Jesus Christ. In Jesus Most

Holy name, we pray, Amen.

Text

Our text today is taken from Paul's letter to the Romans:

How, then, can they call on him they have not believed in? And how can they believe without hearing about him? And how can they hear without a preacher? And how can they preach unless they are sent? As it is written, how beautiful are the feet of those who bring good news.

Textual Idea

Today's text leads us to two questions: (#1) How can people come to know the saving grace of Jesus Christ without someone telling them? And (#2) who is being sent to share the good news?

Sermon Idea/Proposition

The main idea of today's message is "every believer, man or woman has a calling to serve God with their life, so where is God calling you?

Need

Today in North America there are over 281 million people who do not know Jesus; that is three out of four people, including people you know, friends, coworkers and maybe someone even living with you at the same address. More than ever as the body of Christ, every Christian needs to realize God has a call on each individual's life to share Jesus to a lost and broken world.

Interrogative

As so many need to learn and know of Jesus, the standing question is, how and where is God calling you to serve and proclaim him?

Division Statement 1: (Our first main question of the day)
What is the Story God Wants You to Hear and Share?
Explanation

As we explore today's Scripture, let's take a moment to briefly scan and review this letter Paul wrote to the Romans leading up to today's text in chapter 10. This portion of Scripture is well known, as it has been used as an evangelism tool also known as the Romans Road providing a very clear message. This was Paul's way in his time, similar to a newspaper boy shouting out "read all about it!" to shout out the headline, "Jesus is Alive!" He is arisen from the dead!

Paul may have not been a newspaper editor, but not unlike the editors of today he knew how to write a story with a compelling headline and a byline and explained the story in detail. He communicated clearly "those who repent of their sins and fully believe and trust in Jesus will receive the gift of eternal life."

Let's look at the context of the situation. Paul had not yet to visit Rome when he wrote this letter to the Romans in 57 AD. He was on the final leg of his stay in the ancient city of Corinth, which was located in Greece on an isthmus separating the Aegean Sea and the Ionian Sea, which were only six miles apart. It was there Paul would have seen firsthand the depravity of the human condition, as it was a place where there would be everyday encounters with sailors, tradesman, idolators, and even enslaved Christians. Sexual immorality was rampant. There was a temple dedicated to the goddess Aphrodite, and young women would serve as prostitutes in tribute to this goddess of fertility. The combination of Paul's experience and interactions in Corinth aided him in writing his letter to Romans, as he could truly relate, possessing a firsthand perspective of their situation.

So now we have the context, let's join Paul as we quickly scan the highlights of this Roman Road. In the first portion of chapter 1, Paul details his qualifications to proclaim the gospel to everyone. Paul wrote he was set apart to do so to preach the message itself, the gospel, and was eager to preach it in Rome. He wrote:

For I am not ashamed of the gospel, because it is the power of salvation to everyone who believes, first to the Jew, and also the Greek. For in it the righteousness of God is revealed from faith to faith, just as it is written: The righteous will live by faith. (Rom 1:16–17)

So, what is this one true gospel Paul is writing about? To find out, let's look at John 10.

In John 10 Jesus said, "I am the gate. If anyone enters by me, he will be saved." The gospel we are to trust is the gate to salvation, which is Jesus Christ himself. We are to sincerely repent of our sins, and Christ will forgive our transgressions as he himself atoned for our sins on the cross. Very simply, this is the gospel! This is the power of salvation, and this is the story God wants us to hear and share.

Now if you have never heard of the Roman Road or understood this evangelistic method to explain the gospel, then I encourage you to take careful notes. Today, we are going to outline the key truths.

Truth One (All have Sinned). The passage to correlate with this is Romans 3:23 where Paul provided the reason we all need to be saved: "For all have sinned and fall short of the glory of God. They are justified freely by his grace through the redemption that is in Christ Jesus." We can only receive this gift through faith.

Truth Two (Understanding the Consequences of Sin). (Rom 6:23a) "For the wages of sin is death. Then Paul continues in the second part of this verse:

Truth Three (God's Gift). (Rom 6:23b) "but the gift of God is eternal life in Christ Jesus our Lord."

Truth Four (God's Love). (Rom 5:8) "But God proves his own love for us in that while we were still sinners, Christ died for us."

Truth Five (Our Response). (Rom 10:9–11) "If you confess with your mouth, "Jesus is Lord," and believe in your heart that God raised him from the dead, you will be saved. One believes with the heart, resulting in righteousness, and one confesses with the mouth resulting in salvation. For the Scripture says, "Everyone who believes on him will not be put to shame."

Truth Six (Eternal Assurance). Paul quotes the prophet Joel in Romans 10:13: "For everyone who calls on the name of Jesus will be saved."

Here is the succinct summary of these steps: we are sinful and desperate for salvation, there is only one who has justified us with the gift of righteousness, and that is Jesus. We are to repent, confess our sins, and turn away from all unrighteousness and follow Jesus. He is our only hope.

Illustration

The best way to illustrate how desperate our need is for salvation is to imagine a group of people rafting down a raging river. They are proud and strong—all strong swimmers—and rather than wear their life jackets, they leave them on floor of their raft. While rafting, a torrential downpour of rain falls upon them and the river begins to swell and rages even more. They are bounced along the waves, and gripping their paddles they encounter a narrow place in the river where the current is swift and rocks abound everywhere. All of the sudden the raft capsizes, and everyone is thrown from the boat. Their life preservers are swept away out of reach, the river is swollen, and the current and undertows are at what seems full speed. Everyone needs rescued, and behind them comes another craft with experienced rafters wearing their life vests, and they have a round life preserver. Those whom they can reach are saved, and those they cannot reach are taken down by the grip of river and are forever lost. The only hope to remain alive was to grab and hold on to the life preserver. This story a strong parallel to our story, our only hope is Jesus!

Argumentation

The truth found in these series of Bible verses is very clear. We have all fallen short of the glory of God; we have all sinned and deserve death. And even though you and I are mired deep within our sin, Jesus took the cross for us that we may be saved to live with him in eternity. We are to confess, repent, turn away from all unrighteousness, and follow him. He is our only hope. This is where the rubber meets the road for each of us; this is where you have to make a decision. Do you admit you are sinful?

Application

The good news to share is that Jesus died on the cross for our sins, and because of him we are made clean in his righteousness. We know this as the church in Corinth knew this, as Paul wrote in his second letter to the Corinthians: "He made the one who did not know sin to be sin for us, so that in we might become the righteousness of God" (2 Cor 5:21). There is no way we make ourselves clean and righteous without Jesus. The writer of Hebrews noted that Jesus is the new covenant, and all those who place their trust in Jesus Christ share in the eternal inheritance Jesus provides through his death and resurrection. He is our redeemer—your redeemer and my redeemer and we are only made pure by his blood that Christ himself provided by his redemption. It is only because of his blood and sacrifice that our sins are atoned for each of us and we share in the salvation he provides.

Transition

This is the good news for all to hear, but how can one know the gospel without hearing it? This leads us to our next question.

Division Statement 2:
How Can God's Story Be Told without a Preacher?
Explanation

As we reflect on this question and the calling of the apostle Paul, a quick reference to reflect upon is Acts 9, where Paul has his encounter on the Damascus Road. Prior to this chapter, we learn that Paul, then known by his Hebrew name Saul, had just overseen the stoning and death of Stephen. And now in chapter 9, still in a rage Saul requested letters from the Jewish leadership to arrest Christ followers, known as "The Way," in the city of Damascus. He was a very driven man, and I believe from reading the Scriptures he and those with him would have swiftly walked—maybe even marched—feeling unstoppable with incredible zeal as he had orders in hand. It was as they were marching when all of the sudden "boom!" Jesus stopped Saul dead in his tracks, blinding him, and Jesus spoke to him in a very clear voice: "Saul, why are you persecuting me?" In response, the shaken Saul remarked, "Who are you, Lord?" In response Jesus said, "I am Jesus the one you are persecuting. . . . 'But get up and go into the city, and you will be told what you must do.' And all those with him could hear the voice of Jesus." It was then that Saul the persecutor got up off his hands and knees and finished his journey to Damascus blind. We turn the page to the next scene in the story, Damascus, where the Lord spoke to a man named Ananias.

> *There was a disciple in Damascus named Ananias, the Lord said to him in a vision, "Ananias."*
> *"Here I am, Lord," he replied.*
> *"Get up and go to the street called Straight," the Lord said to him, "to the house of Judas and ask for a man from Tarsus named Saul, since he is praying there. In a vision he has seen a man named Ananias coming in and placing his hands on him so that he may regain his sight."*
> *"Lord," Anaias answered, "I have heard from many people about this man, how much harm he has done to your saints in Jerusalem. And he has authority here from the chief priests to arrest all who call on your name."*
> *But the Lord said to him, "Go for this man is my chosen instrument to take my name to the Gentiles, kings, and Israelites. I will show him how much he must suffer for my name." (Acts 9:10–16)*

Obviously, Ananias was reticent, yet he was obedient to the Lord and upon Ananias's entry into the house where Saul was located, the miraculous was about to take place. Ananias placed his hands upon Saul, he was filled with the Holy Spirit, scales fell off his eyes, and he was then baptized. It was an amazing transformation as Saul made a complete 180 degree turn around because in verse 19 we learn that Saul remained in Damascus for some time, not as a persecutor but as a strong advocate proclaiming Jesus as the Lord and Messiah.

So, why share this account with you today? I share it for you to realize God's story is to be told! His story needs to be told by a preacher. I share with you today because it is a great example of how God can use anyone, anytime, anywhere for his purpose. Your whole life you could be living off the rails, and if God so chooses you, just like Paul, you too can be a chosen instrument for his service. Today, the Holy Spirit could be using my voice to speak to you. God has a plan for each of us, what is his plan for you?

Illustration

There are many stories of men who had other plans for their life and God changed the trajectory of their lives. Peter Ko was a student from Korea attending the University of Oregon to study medicine to become a doctor when God spin him around, and now he is a pastor of a Korean-speaking church in Madison, Wisconsin. Reggie Taylor is from Memphis, Tennessee; he dropped out of school at age 13. Reggie was moving one to two kilos of cocaine and two hundred pounds of weed every week, and he was snorting fifteen to twenty grams of cocaine each day. As he explains in his own words, he was a drug doer, a drug distributor, and a drug dealer. He had been locked up five times, and in January 1992, while he was locked up, he overheard the gospel message and started reading the Bible. A year later, in July 1993, as Reggie explained to me, the Lord made it very clear that he had a call to preach the good news. Today he is a pastor in South Haven, Mississippi. Grant Gaines grew up in a Christian home and felt the call of ministry as an aspiration when he was thirteen years old. During his high school years, he was given opportunities to teach and to preach, and it was during this time his calling was affirmed. Grant entered seminary because he felt like that is what God wanted him to do, and today he pastors a church in Murfreesboro, Tennessee. God can call anyone, anywhere, anytime, and he can use a man or he can use a woman and he can use you.

Argumentation

Paul was on the Damascus Road; he was considered enemy number one by all those who claimed Christ, and God turned him around. Peter Ko was planning a career in medicine and God placed him on a completely different path. Reggie Taylor by all accounts was a complete drop out of proper society, but God picked him up, cleaned him up, and now he is a proper man of God on fire, a disciple maker preaching the gospel message. Grant Gaines grew up in a strong Christian home, and he like many men with similar stories remained faithful and true, and God is actively using him for his service. The point is, God needs a preacher to tell his story! It doesn't matter if you were a murderer like Saul, a former drug dealer like Reggie, someone who has their whole life mapped out like Peter Ko, or if every piece of the puzzle is in place due to your upbringing and faithfulness like Grant Gaines, God has a plan! He can use anyone from anywhere, from any circumstance to be his chosen instrument.

Application

The Bible is filled with examples of faithful men God called to fulfill his purpose. We see this throughout the Old Testament, and in Hebrews 11 the writer posted the short list of the faithful. Look at all these people from humble beginnings whom God used. Noah who was warned about what was to come built an ark, then Abraham who was called by God, and although he had his shortcomings, is known throughout history for his faithfulness. Then there is Moses: he was eighty years old when God called him, and what amazing life he lived! Think about the prostitute Rahab who welcomed the spies entering Jericho in peace and did not disobey, and she was blessed to be a mother in Jesus's lineage. Then there were David, Samson, Gideon, and so many others. When you look in the mirror reflect on where you have been in your life, your personal character, the deeds you have done, and you do not feel worthy, remember this: it is God who does the calling. He is the one who deems who is worthy. You may not be called to ministry leadership, but all of us are called to do the work of ministry. In Ephesians 4 Paul wrote,

"And he himself gave some to be apostles, some prophets, some evangelists, some pastors and teachers, equipping the saints for the work of ministry to build-up the body of Christ" (Eph 4:11).

The pastors and teachers do the equipping, but all are called. That means every Christian is called for the work of ministry. You may not be called to be an evangelist who speaks before large crowds or a pastor or a teacher, but God has called you to serve, to care for others using your gifts for everyday evangelism. If you are a woman, God may be calling you to be a missionary or a teacher; if you are man God may be calling you like he has called so many others to preach the Word and share the Good News of Jesus Christ. You see, God can use anyone, anywhere, anytime!

Transition

God calls preachers to tell his story, which leads to the question: Who is going to be sent by God to tell the story?

Division Statement 3:
Who Is Going to Be Sent by God to Tell the Story?
Explanation

Throughout the ages God has sent men to tell his story. Those sent have been men who are fearful and even harbor hatred toward those God intends to save. One such person was Jonah. God called him to preach repentance to the citizens of Nineveh. Jonah lived in the Northern Kingdom of Israel, and he like others in his society held hatred in his heart for the people of Nineveh. But God chose Jonah, and as many of us know Jonah turned away, jumping on a ship to escape from this assignment. As the ship was in the middle of the sea, a storm raged as Jonah slept in the bowels of the ship. The captain of the ship awoke Jonah and asked him to call upon God to stop the storm. Of all things, Jonah convinced the men to throw him into the sea to stop the storm, which miraculously happened, and God sent a fish that swallowed up Jonah. In his distress while in the belly of the fish, he prayed for God's hand on his life, and the fish spewed Jonah out onto dry land. It was there, once again, that God called Jonah to preach the message repentance to the people of Nineveh. It was a three-day walk, and Jonah preached and the people turned from evil and worshiped the Lord. Even after the king and the people of Nineveh repented and turned from their ways, Jonah was upset with God because of the hatred for the people of Nineveh that persisted in his heart. Jonah stormed off into the heat of desert and God created a plant to shade him, and even then, Jonah held evil in his heart, waiting to watch the demise of the city. God caused the plant to die, and Jonah lamented about the death of the plant. It was then that God in conversation with Jonah made a very strong point with this angry prophet. God remarked how Jonah cared so much about a plant that grew in a night and died in a night, so how is it that he, God the Father, should not care about the 120,000 people in Nineveh? What a story and what a lesson for you and me in our age!

Who are the people God cares about and who need to hear the words of a preacher? Who is he going to send? I believe there is someone here today that God is calling; maybe that someone is you. You see, God can use anyone, anywhere, anytime!

Illustration

Upon mentioning the letters IRS or even saying the words Internal Revenue Service we will all have that uneasy feeling, as paying taxes and dealing with IRS is not the most pleasant task. In Jesus's day, the Jewish people had a great disdain for the tax collectors. The tax collectors worked for the Roman government, and they would collect the tribute that was required, and to pay themselves they would add what you and I would call a surtax, a tax on the tax. Many tax collectors became very wealthy by extorting people and were so disliked and in many cases became estranged even from their own families.

A tax collector would not seem to be the most likely candidate to be allowed into Jesus's inner circle. However, it was Matthew to whom Jesus said the words, "Follow me!" And at once Matthew walked away from the toll booth, leaving a life of privilege and wealth to walk with one who would provide him eternal riches. Matthew was probably the intellectually smartest of all the twelve disciples. Experts note that because of his craft as a tax collector, Matthew would have probably known seven different languages and of course would have possessed mathematical acumen. The point is, Jesus can call anyone from any walk of life from anywhere and anytime to be in his service. The question at hand is this… What is Jesus calling you to do? You see, God can use anyone, and he can use you!

Argumentation

Looking upon the life of Jonah and those God is calling to tell his story; it is clear that God has a purpose for every believer's life. Jonah in the belly of the fish confessed to God that salvation belongs to the Lord, and when he was spewed out, he kept his vow and quickly made his way to Nineveh, proclaiming for everyone to call upon the one true God. Jonah was the herald of his time, look around—who in your midst is the herald of our time? Is it you? God can call anyone, anywhere, anytime.

Application

The application for you and me is to realize there are three calls. The first is the call to salvation. The second is the call to sanctification and service. And finally, the third call is to ministry leadership. Perhaps upon examining your life you realize that today is the day to place your full trust in Jesus as your Lord and Savior. And by proclaiming your faith, there may be others within your sphere upon witnessing your confession, that may also be affected by your witness and believe, trust in Jesus.

Maybe there are some of you here who are like Jonah. God has been calling you to serve and minister others, but rather than step up, it has always seemed easier to walk away. Today may be the day you realize that God needs your talent and gifts to help others. In the Sermon on the Mount, Jesus taught that no one lights a lamp and puts it under a basket but rather on a lampstand to give to light to everyone in the house. How can you use your gifts to be a light and share the gospel story? Perhaps it is visiting those people who are shut-ins and others in the nursing homes. Maybe you have a special talent to help with young people or small children. Maybe your talent is helping to counsel others; maybe it is to help someone with fixing up around their house and while doing so... sharing the light of Jesus's love. There is a multiplicity of ways to serve and, everyone who is a Christian is a minister of Christ. You have a special talent that can be used.

Today, maybe you realize God is calling you into ministry leadership. You may have known for a long time and have this internal desire to serve and share the gospel. Maybe you have experienced conversation with others who have shared they see something special in you, yet you have not placed your "Yes" on the table. Maybe you have been serving as a teacher, a counselor, or encourager and you have sensed the Holy Spirit stirring within your soul. It could be that you have been praying for direction and were waiting for a nudge. Maybe you possess such an unsettled feeling of what you are doing now and realize God has other plans. Perhaps it is time to travel down a new road and discover a new journey. God has a plan for your life, and you do not want to miss your calling.

Transition to Conclusion

The message has made clear there is a story that God wants everyone to hear, a preacher is needed to tell the story and herald the message, and finally the preacher must be sent.

Conclusion/Invitation

Every man and woman mentioned today was on journey: Noah, Abraham, Moses, Rahab Jonah, Peter Ko, Reginald Taylor, and Grant Gaines. God used the men of old, and these living men of today . . . He is still using people to tell his story. There are men and women today in our midst whom God is using, and God is stirring in their hearts right now to serve him. Maybe that someone is you. Perhaps you are a man and have an aspiration to serve in ministry leadership, and you wonder if God is calling you. Maybe you are a woman and you want to dedicate your life to the service of God in the mission field, uplifting other women or helping children and youth of all ages to the saving knowledge of Jesus. Maybe you are a pastor and you know you should be more intentional about identifying men for service. Maybe you are deacon or leader in the church and there is someone you know you should have an "I see in you" conversation to encourage a person that God has placed upon your heart. Maybe there is a person known to everyone here today wrestling with the call to ministry and they are truly called and just need your affirmation. Are you the parent of a child who lacks confidence and feels there is no way they can serve God in the capacity of the high office of pastor and you see something in them that they cannot see? Today is the day to have that conversation! Today is the day of action! God can call anyone from anywhere, any place, and anytime . . . that anytime could be right now. Don't miss this! If God is calling you, today is the day to come forward. If there is someone who needs your affirmation, today is the day to make a commitment. If you are a pastor and you need to pray for God to bless your ministry tree, today is the day; don't miss this! It was Isaiah who wrote: "Then I heard the voice of the Lord asking: Who should I send? Who will go for us? I said: Here I am. Send me."

2 Timothy 2:1-2 Call-to-Ministry Message

Introduction

Today we are going to talk about teaching others who teach others. I bet in every family represented here today there are many great teachers. Let me explain. My grandparents on my mother's side were second-generation German immigrants who settled in southern Indiana. My great-grandmother Mary Waldkoetter made the most delicious yeast rolls; she handed off the recipe to my Grandmother Lillian, who later owned and operated a restaurant famous for her pies and yeast rolls. My mother Judy was a home economics teacher and catered and was known for her amazing yeast rolls. I am the oldest of five, and my sister Marg in particular has the family recipe down pat; she never makes a bad batch! My granddaughter Ellie loves to bake with my sister, and there is great hope she too will continue the family tradition. She would account for five known generations of bakers. I would wager that in your family there is some special skill that has been handed down through the generations. Today, we are going to talk about sharing one of the most important lessons to pass along with others, including our family, friends, coworkers and even complete strangers, and that is the eternal hope found in the gospel message of Jesus Christ.

Prayer

So let's begin our day with prayer:

Dear Heavenly Father,

This day we ask for your power to work through our lives to reach those within our realm with the gospel message of salvation. We pray for diligence amongst everyone here today to be bold and unashamed to share the joy we all share in knowing Jesus Christ is our Lord and Savior. In Jesus's Most

Holy name, we pray, Amen.

Text

Our text today is:

> "You, therefore, my son, be strong in the grace that is in Christ Jesus. What you have heard from me in the presence of many witnesses, commit to faithful men who will able to teach others also." (2 Timothy 2:1–2).

Textual Idea

Paul wrote to Timothy to be strong in grace and what he had heard from him, to teach others also.

Sermon Idea/Proposition

My goal for you today is to take hold of your responsibility as disciple makers to make a commitment to identify, encourage and invest in capable men and women to share the gospel message.

Need

The need is obvious as our culture is besieging our families. Every day we live on the frontlines in a culture war of right and wrong and good versus evil. In reality it is a war between heaven and hell! Now is the time that requires believers to take a stand for our faith.

Interrogative

So, the first question of the day is, where do you stand in sharing your faith? To whom have you shared your faith in the past week or month? To whom are you committed to teach so they too will teach others?

Division Statement 1: (First Insight)
Commit to Be Strong in Grace Found in Christ
Explanation

Today, we are going to explore our text, 2 Timothy 2:1–2. This is the second letter written to Timothy and Paul's final letter. Many Bible scholars claim this letter Paul's last will and testament. During the time of Paul's first imprisonment, he was under house arrest and free to preach. We know this from Acts 28:31, where Luke wrote, "Paul stayed two whole years in his own rented house. And he welcomed all who visited him, proclaiming the kingdom of God and teaching about the Lord Jesus with all boldness and without hindrance."

While writing this second letter to Timothy, things were the complete opposite of that situation and dramatically different for the apostle, as was then he was in a Roman prison cell. He would have been in chains, sharing his cell with others, and incarcerated without much light and most likely very primitive sanitation. It would have been an awful situation, and Paul knew his fate as Emperor Nero was on a rampage. Nero had burned down his own city, the capital city of his empire—Rome—and used the Christians as a scapegoat. The apostle Paul as the leader of this movement faced certain death. It was a moment when Paul absolutely leaned into his faith, fully embracing the grace of the Lord Jesus Christ to overcome the plight of his day-to-day existence. Hopefully, this provides each of you with some context for this letter.

The main themes of this letter were to encourage Timothy 1) to follow Jesus even when things get difficult, and 2) to cling to the faith and hope in Jesus's resurrection. Paul challenged Timothy to adhere to strong doctrine and oppose false teaching. He shared that suffering is part of the Christian experience, to preserve the Scriptures, and for Timothy to acknowledge he would endure hardship and should recognize the significance of diligence in service. And finally, Paul told Timothy that no matter what happens in the world, Jesus . . . Jesus is the rock of our salvation.

So, what does it mean to commit to being strong in grace found in Christ? It means as believers it's about finding your strength not in yourself but in the unconditional love and grace that Jesus Christ offers. It's a commitment to let grace guide you through life's challenges, to accept that you're imperfect but loved, and to show that same grace to others. It's a transformative journey, relying on faith rather than personal ability. John wrote, "Indeed, we have all received grace upon grace from his fullness, for the law was given through Moses; grace came through Jesus Christ" (John 1:16–17).

I love this verse! Grace upon grace is a constant, overflowing gift for all of us who know Jesus. We received that gift the day when Jesus was scourged, beaten, and crucified on the cross and died to cover the penalty for our sins. It is to fully embrace the knowledge of our salvation that delivered us from the dire straits of our sin. Grace upon grace is to admonish ourselves to show, display, and exhibit love to others. It is to love those who have hurt or betrayed us and those whose actions have caused us harm. It is to love our family when we don't want to love our family, to love our coworkers, friends, and neighbors when we feel they mistreat us. It is to love our enemies and to love our neighbors as Jesus loved us. Paul wrote that the law was revealed by Moses, showing us our sins, but our true redemption has been provided through the love and grace of Jesus Christ our Savior. Let me share a true-life story as an example of true forgiveness, redemption, and what it means to be strong in grace.

Illustration

Bruce Murakami is a man who displayed remarkable grace, so much so that they made a Hallmark movie showcasing the story of his family. In 1998, Bruce's wife Cindy and his eleven-year-old daughter Chelsea had gone to the store when something tragic unfolded. A nineteen-year-old young man named Justin Cabezas was a teen street racer in Tampa, Florida, and he slammed into their minivan. The minivan had exploded into flames and was an inferno. Bruce had seen smoke from his house and had an intuition to see the source of the smoke. It was something normally he would not do. Bruce drove to the scene of the accident, where tragically he witnessed the deaths of his wife and daughter. He and his two sons were deeply grieved, and Bruce spent three years and thousands of dollars seeking justice for the death of his wife and daughter. Finally, the court charged Justin Cabezas with vehicular homicide. It was then that Bruce had a major change of heart after seeing Justin in a different light for the very first time. Justin reminded him of his sons, and rather than see him behind bars, Bruce pleaded for mercy to the judge on behalf of driver who killed his wife and daughter. Rather than sentencing Justin to prison thirty years, he pleaded for the judge for an alternative plan to have him do community service—a very special kind of community service. Justin was to join Bruce traveling to schools to give talks to student assemblies on the importance of safe student driving.

Argumentation

In the story I just shared, please know Bruce was a strong Christian, he had read his Bible front to back, he was faithful, and he knew Jesus. He, like most of us if we had experienced such a tragedy, was at first very angry with God. He went to the beach to sit every day to reflect, and during the duration of his grief it became obvious to him that he was going to become the third victim. Bruce finally picked up his Bible again and upon reading Luke 6, he decided to forgive Justin. He decided to be strong in grace and rely on the power of Jesus rather than upon his own strength and understanding. Bruce's story is a perfect picture of this truth. There is no way in our carnal flesh that we can always be strong and do the right thing without the power of God. It requires us to lean on the Lord, to lean into His Word, which is His will, and pray and ask for his power to help us stand upright. It is not always easy to do. Hopefully, most of us will not experience the tragedy like Bruce Murakami and his family faced, but his story shows that we must commit to be strong in grace.

Application

To be strong in faith means as a Christian we need to more than look like one; rather, we need to *be* one. What does that look like? It means as believers we truly practice all the spiritual disciplines or what Donald Whitney, professor at Midwestern Seminary and author of a book on spiritual disciplines, calls "habits of devotion." We take time every day to read our Bible, we take time to pray by ourselves and with others, we read the Scriptures, we work on memorizing the Word. As we memorize the Word it becomes a part of us. We practice godliness and confess our sins and ask for repentance. In our relations with others, we share the Word; and when we encounter difficulties with others, we exhibit our best behavior and decide to choose forgiveness. We choose to practice the charitable traits, as Paul wrote to the Colossians, of compassion, kindness, gentleness, humility, and patience with others. When we face tough circumstances and challenges, we fall to our knees and ask the Holy Spirit to do a major work in our hearts to transform us so we do not conform to the pattern of the world but are transformed by the renewing of our minds. Paul deeply knew and practiced his faith as he was deeply remorseful for his past sins. Upon encountering Jesus, he discovered a newfound faith that did not preclude him from experiencing true suffering. As he preached the truth, those who rejected it attempted to do him harm and even kill him. He was stoned, beaten, whipped, placed on trial, shipwrecked, and faced the penalty of a physical death. Even through all those circumstances he had not lost his faith as he wrote to Timothy: be strong in the grace of that is in Christ Jesus.

Transition

Please know Jesus is the one to whom we can totally rely upon, it makes no difference our experience as Jesus is our one true treasure and in him can be found our eternal assurance.

Division Statement 2: (Second Insight)
Commit to Listen and Study the Word of God
Explanation

In Acts 16:3, Paul chose Timothy. He was an obvious choice because he was active in the church, exhibiting character and leadership traits. Moreover, Timothy had studied the Word from a young age. As we reflect upon his life, scholars know Timothy's father was a Greek, a Gentile, and he would have learned the Scriptures from his mother who was Jewish. In the context of first-century Jewish tradition, a child began his religious training at age five and would continue until twelve or thirteen years of age; obviously his mother and grandmother provided him the traditional religious education necessary to be part of Jewish society. Studying and learning the Word was taken very seriously during Timothy's age.

Now in our day, according to Lifeway Research, only about 34 percent of Americans read the Bible at least once a week, while 50 percent—or one-half—of Americans read something in the Bible only twice a year. In Lifeway's 2019 study, 78 percent of pastors indicated a need to improve discipleship in their church. It is the pastor's role to set the tone for discipleship in their church. Not to be condemning, but is this happening? In my church this is happening and people are growing spiritually and we are growing in numbers. The challenge is for the people to embrace the importance of studying the Scriptures. The best way to know the Word is to study alongside others. A good recommendation is to choose three or four other people and commit to read a Bible plan together. We need to be encouraging for all generations to read the Bible, from the Alpha Generation to Baby Boomers. It is best if a group comprised of either all males or all females and hold one another accountable to read the Bible daily and memorize Scriptures. We need to embrace the adage, get into the Word until the Word gets into you.

Illustration

When I was in high school in southern Indiana and my first several years of college, I had a burning desire to farm. I worked on a truck farm one summer and awoke at 3:25 a.m. to make it to the field by 4 a.m., early in the morning every day in July to pick sweet corn. We would walk down rows of wet, dew-laden corn. I realized it really wasn't my idea of fun. The next summer, I worked with Fred and Philip Pottschmidt. I drove tractors and we planted corn, put up hay, straw, and silage. Fred had an eighty-head cow herd and a two-hundred-head cattle feedlot, so I got to learn a lot about cattle. I subscribed to *Successful Farming Magazine* and *Drovers Journal*; I immersed myself with learning about the latest cultural practices to increase crop yields and raise livestock. I self-taught myself and took an extra class with farmers to learn about technical analysis in marketing. I charted the markets daily, including the high, low, and close of day for the future markets. In doing so, I shared with Fred there was key reversal in the charts. In technical analysis, it is a signal the market is going to change. The chart showed the cattle price was at the top, the high of the market. I showed it to Fred, and he took two loads of cattle to the market in Louisville and got the high price. He was so happy, and I was never so proud. The point of sharing all of this is when it comes to something we love or have interest in knowing—we go all out! In the same way, to grow ourselves spiritually and become closer to God, it is vital to dig into the Word. As we study with others, we will be transformed and discover a key reversal in our own lives.

Argumentation

As we commit to listen and study the Word of God, we begin to grow in not just in the knowledge of our God—Father, Son and Holy Spirit—we begin to grow in our faith. This knowledge is like a seed that begins to grow within us. It causes us to want to read, study, learn, and share with others. This thirst to know more of God becomes like a hunger, and we listen to a greater variety of those of speak God's Word. Paul chose Timothy as his protégé because he witnessed his desire to learn, his desire to grow, and perhaps noticed a little of himself in Timothy, including Paul's tenacity. As Paul, Silas, and Timothy sailed across the Aegean Sea, can you imagine their excitement to share the gospel? And can you imagine their conversations while traveling along well-worn walking paths? Timothy would have been like a sponge listening to Paul's insights and lessons about Scripture. Fast-forward, and we learn of Timothy's tenacity in Hebrews 13:23, as the writer revealed Timothy had been jailed: "Be aware that our brother Timothy has been released. If he comes soon enough, he will be with me when I see you." Like Paul, Timothy was unyielding in his faith. It is apparent Timothy took to heart the words in this letter to commit to listen and study the Word of God. And that is a reminder for us all.

Application

The application for you and me is very clear: we need to take every opportunity to listen to the Word of God. We need to make it a priority! The priority is that we need to make weekly attendance in corporate worship a non-negotiable. We need to listen and study beyond one hour on Sunday morning. In our age we have multiple resources available at our fingertips. Technology allows us to hear the message of God from many voices by pushing a couple buttons or making a few clicks. Just think about all the options to grow in the knowledge of God. We can show up at church, listen on a variety of social media platforms, turn on our television or listen on the radio, read our Bibles or pick up a Christian book or magazine and begin reading. I want to encourage you if you are not already, to join a D-Group, that is, a discipleship group, and choose a Bible reading plan and meet weekly on a consistent basis. Take time to study the Word in your home with your family and pray with them. If you are married, pray daily with your wife. There are a boundless array of studies and resources available today for each of us; there are no excuses why we cannot commit to listen and study the Word of God.

Think about this: for those us who make it a priority to walk or run every day, or make it to the gym multiple times a week, after a period of time you begin to see results. The more you study and listen to the Word of God, the more you take time for prayer and meditation upon his Word, the more likely you begin to see your faith grow, your prayer life grow, your thoughts and words change. It will affect the way you relate with others, and you will begin to think more upon the things of God versus man. You will begin to experience a new joy found from truly understanding the love of Jesus in your heart as you commit to listen and study the Word.

Transition

Paul chose Timothy because he was grounded in his faith and because Timothy knew knowing God and studying his Word would enable him to be able to teach others too.

Division Statement 3: (Our third insight)
Commit to Faithful Men Who Will Teach Others
Explanation

As we reflect upon Acts 16, Timothy begins a new chapter in his life as Paul witnessed in him traits essential to propagate the gospel message. He possessed the necessary disposition and temperament, and this is first observed in his willingness to be circumcised as to be more accepted by those with a Jewish background. This was definitely a sign of his faithfulness. The lesson to be learned is God only gives out assignments when we have the character to match it. The elders in the church of Lystra and Derbe knew Timothy's character, and God chose in his timing the next step in his spiritual journey. Paul ordained him into service, as noted in 1 Timothy 4:14. Just as Paul chose Timothy for his faithfulness, he chose him for his willingness to learn and develop his ability to teach. Timothy willingly accepted many ministry roles involving teaching others, including following Paul to serve as a pastor in some pretty tough places, most notably in the cities of Corinth and Ephesus, which were not necessarily the most Christian-friendly places.

Twenty-one centuries later the significance of finding faithful men to pastor and teach others is still paramount. There is similarity in time past and today. In Paul's day the fledging church was just beginning to take root and most of the world knew little of Jesus. Now in our day, we live in a time of a postmodern Christianity. It is now a time where everyone who claims Jesus just like those in the first century is a missionary. We are missionaries as soon as we leave the house or maybe inside of our very own homes. In the Scriptures there is a list of thirty-one coworkers who assisted the apostle Paul. He was always seeking faithful men and women to aide in propagating the gospel message to the world. He was able to enlist these individuals to reach the Greco-Roman world. At the same time, the disciples who walked with Jesus were reaching Jews and Gentiles in Israel and Samaria. Together as coworkers they shared the gospel and turned the world upside down. They did all this without the modern methods and means we have today.

Illustration

As a young boy I delivered the *Louisville Courier Journal* in my hometown. I would arise in the wee hours in the morning—dark in the winter and lighter in the summer—to prepare and make my daily trip around town on my bicycle. The circulation manager decided to choose me because my dad convinced him I would do a good job and was responsible. Mind you, I was only ten years old. The circulation manager's job was to enlist the aid of newspaper delivery persons all over southern Indiana. I was not the only one delivering the daily news and the messages contained in those papers. It required as a corps of individuals young and old who could be trusted to follow through each and every day in multiple cities and towns both large and small. The circulation manager was entrusted with teaching others, and my job was to follow through.

Argumentation

In the same way, Paul entrusted Timothy to deliver the good news, and Timothy was to find other men who could deliver the good news. This has continued for generations. Just like my opening story of the generation of bakers making rolls in my family, in order to keep the tradition going, it has to handed down to another who will do the same. Likewise, it is imperative to find faithful men to teach others to perpetuate the delivery of the good news. Jesus had many individuals who followed him. These followers watched him and learned from him. Jesus chose those who were teachable and those who would be able to share the gospel with the world.

We learn this from Luke 6:

> *During those days he went out to the mountain to pray and spent all night in prayer to God. When daylight came, he summoned his disciples, and he chose twelve of them, whom he also named apostles: Simon, whom he*

also named Peter, and Andrew his brother; James and John; Philip and Bartholomew; Matthew and Thomas; James the son of Alphaeus, and Simon called the Zealot; Judas the son of James, and Judas Iscariot, who became a traitor. (Luke 6:12–16)

Application

In 2025, the average age of a pastor in the United States is sixty-one. There are literally thousands of people in counties across America who do not attend church and who do not know Jesus. As we gaze upon our culture and the issues of the day, it is evident we live in a world nearly blind to Christ. It is for this reason we need a revival of discipleship in our churches. It is also important for our pastors to identify men in their midst who can be developed and mentored to assume leadership roles in the church. Jesus developed his disciples before selecting the twelve; in the same manner pastors should consider men who are suitable and qualified to teach to walk alongside them. My ministry mentor and colleague Tim LaFleur shares the following model as the perfect model presented by Jesus for discipleship:

- Jesus did it and disciples watched.
- Jesus did it and discipled assisted.
- The disciples did it and Jesus assisted.
- The disciples did it and Jesus watched.

Jesus modeled the work of ministry for his disciples to follow; we are to do the same today!

As we look in our congregations and evaluate the men in our midst, no matter their ages, some young in their teens or twenties, maybe in their thirties or forties, or perhaps older in their fifties and sixties, we must realize that God has a place for them. He has a place where they can lay their "yes" on the table. My prayer is that pastors will walk with these men to help support them and assist them to grow into spiritual maturity. I pray for our pastors to be bold and to have "I see in you" conversations with these men. Conversations that may sound like this: I see in you an ability to connect with others, an internal desire to serve and care for people, and a real hunger to grow deeper in your relationship with the Lord. Upon having these conversations, it is important to encourage these men to seek God in prayer and ask for his will to be done. It is also important that pastors provide opportunities for these men to walk alongside of them like Jesus did so they can grow and mature. These men need to be provided opportunities to serve, teach, and even preach to determine if God is calling them.

There is much debate in the church about the role of women in ministry and if they are called to the office of pastor. God does have a calling for women. He calls women to teach other women, young people, and children to help them grow, as well as support and uplift the men in their families. It is also important for the pastor and church leaders to have conversations to uplift these women and provide them with an opportunity for service. It is for certain that women played an integral role in the early church as you look upon the roles of individuals like Priscilla, Phoebe, and Lydia.

Today, look around in your midst. Who do you feel has the qualities for service, a true heart and desire to share Jesus with others? Perhaps it is you! Do you have an aspiration to step up and serve others? Do you have a desire to teach and care for others? Is evangelism in your blood and you cannot help but want to share Jesus with the world?

As a church we affirm the calling of men into the ministry. Is there someone you can think of today that perhaps needs your affirmation? It may not mean they are ready today to pastor or preach; it may mean they just need to know "you see in them" the qualities necessary for service. Two questions: Who is that person? And can you be so bold to share an "I see in you" conversation with them? And if they do have an aspiration for ministry leadership to instill in them the need to discern that maybe they are called? Perhaps that person who has an aspiration for ministry leadership is you. I want to encourage you to take a first step and speak with your pastor about what God has laid upon your heart.

Transition to Conclusion

Timothy provided a solid example of being strong in grace and dedicated to studying the Word, and he picked up the torch to enlist faithful men to teach others. His example and Paul's example is our model for today. And we all should be committed as individuals and as a church to follow through to ensure the torch continues to be passed along.

Conclusion/Invitation

Tradition has it that Timothy was martyred in Ephesus when he was over eighty years old. There is not a clear explanation as to how exactly Timothy died; however, based upon various online explanations, it was written in the Apocryphal of Acts of Timothy that he attempted "to put an end to a pagan festival to honor Dionysus in which the participants would dress in costumes, masks and partake in sexual immorality and murder. It was recorded that Timothy exhorted them saying, 'Men of Ephesus do not be mad for idols, but acknowledge the one who truly is God.' Instead of listening to Timothy the revelers attacked and beat him. While Timothy was still barely alive, some fellow Christians took him away from the mob, and when he died, they buried him in a place called Pion in Ephesus." Like Paul, devoted to service, Timothy fought the good fight and finished the race well.

Today, if you feel God is working upon your heart and you feel a sense of calling or an aspiration to serve in ministry leadership, I want you to encourage you to come forward. If you feel a pull on your heart to share Jesus with those who really do not know Christ and you want to figure out the next step, please come forward. Timothy was a young man in his twenties. Maybe you are younger, in your teens; God has called many teenagers. Look at the twelve disciples; nearly everyone was a teenager except for Peter. Perhaps you are older and feel you may have missed your time of calling. You may sense as an older person God can use you. God called Moses when he was eighty, so don't let your age stop you. The Lord may have worked in your life all this time to prepare you for such a moment. He has been shaping and molding you and now is the time . . . He is seeking you to come forward. Maybe you are a woman and you feel God is working in your life to serve in women's ministry, missions, and to share Jesus with youth. If so, please come forward. Maybe God is not calling you into ministry but you sense the Holy Spirit has been working in your heart to share an "I see in you conversation" with someone. If so, then today may be the day to do so. Come forward and make the steps to the altar and pray for boldness. God is working; he is always working, and he is working today in this church. Don't miss it. If you really feel God has been working on your heart to take a step, take that step forward today. Like Paul and Timothy, fight the good fight and finish the race well.

Final Thoughts

Throughout this book we have provided rationale for the importance to focus on the call of ministry. There is a great urgency within the church to raise up men as leaders and to identify those men with a sense of calling to assist them with next steps. The call to ministry is much different than choosing an occupation in a secular field where one desires to work. It requires a supernatural call from God as the Holy Spirit works within a man to provide a burning desire to preach the Word. Our hope is the information contained within these pages has been beneficial to both pastors and those discerning the call to ministry.

We encourage pastors to be intentional to develop leadership training to raise up the next generation of leaders. It is essential to create a formalized discipleship plan and provide a framework for both men and women in the church to grow in their faith and bolster the faith of others within your congregation. There are many avenues to make this happen. We suggest a format of creating small-sized, same-sex discipleship groups consisting of three to four individuals reading through a Bible reading plan and consistently meeting on a regular basis. This action will create a habitual rhythm for both men and women to read the Bible and for disciples to engage one another to grow in their faith while providing a safe place to share challenges and opportunities. The added benefit is as those participating grow in their faith, so does their ability to disciple others promoting spiritual growth within the church and the community.

It is essential for pastors to consider who they can raise up to be their replacement, engaging men to grow as spiritual leaders. Some of these men will learn they are not called to be ministry leadership leaders; others will discover the pull of God is so strong, it is undeniable. It is important to realize the positive benefit of both of these outcomes. We feel strongly the small group Above Reproach process of meeting regularly with men considering the call is invaluable. The process provides a stronghold for men to share and grow in their faith. We encourage working together with other pastors or association leaders to create a more robust environment for a larger group of men to meet to promote interaction and an enriched experience. Our recommendation is to assign a leadership or discipleship book for the participants to read each week and discuss the principles, pray for another, and ask participating pastors questions related to the call process. We also suggest men prepare and present an expositional message based upon a Scripture taken from one of the Pastoral Epistles. This creates a synergistic environment and creates growth opportunities for both the mentee and the mentor.

We are grateful you have taken time to read this book and want to encourage you to share it with others to promote the importance of discipleship, pastoral leadership, and the significance of calling out the called. Finally, we want to encourage you to do your part, whether called to ministry leadership or other ministry roles, to fulfill the Great Commission and make disciples of all nations, starting with your home, your church, and your community.

Your partners in the fellowship of the gospel message,
Rob Millman & Tim LaFleur

Appendices

Appendix A
A Framework for Mentoring Leaders

Framework for an Above Reproach Group

As mentioned previously, I suggested what someone should do, while they discern God's calling on their lives, is to be part of what I call an "Above Reproach" group. This group consists of men who recognize that God is "at work" in their lives and are trying to figure out what He's calling them to and what steps of faith they should take. We believe this group setting can become a "safe place" to share what they believe God is doing in their lives and get feedback as they discern their next steps. Here is a framework for groups that we use.

Intentional Conversation

As group participants arrive, begin a time of intentional conversation. Guys can share their highs and lows (peaks and valleys) with families, jobs, and relationships. It is a time to "catch up" with each other from the last time they met.

Scripture Study

After a time of intentional conversation, ask someone to lead in a brief prayer. Next, I recommend that you study God's Word, beginning with the Pastoral Epistles. Tell the group that you will take the first section of Scripture, then assign others in the group the following sections.

The reason I take the first one is to model before the group how to do inductive Bible study. A principle that I learned years ago is "You can't expect what you do not demonstrate." It's not only important to demonstrate how to do inductive Bible study, but you should teach them how to do it, because they may not be familiar with it. Also, it will be foundational to helping them build a sermon. (Something I teach them after they learn to do inductive Bible study.)

Book Study

After your study of Scripture, spend time reading a book on ministry or church leadership. Read books that have impacted your life and ministry. I will typically ask the guys to read. This allows us to review one chapter per week and take our time to "squeeze" every bit of truth from it. Remember to point out that although the Bible is *essential*, other books can be *helpful*.

Emerging Leader in the Middle

The next part of the meeting is optional. It is what is known as "Emerging Leader in the Middle." As the group grows closer, this can be an effective tool for group members to share what they are struggling with (job, family, next steps, decisions, etc.) and get valuable insight and feedback from the rest of the group. Depending on the size of the group, utilize this tool every week or every other week.

Pray for One Another

Close the meeting by praying for one another. Take time to share gospel-centered prayer request and then pray for one another.

Appendix B

Working Together in Your Association
(Written as a tool for Association Mission Strategists)

Why an Above Reproach Group in Your Church?

As a busy pastor with your many roles and responsibilities, one area that we would like to help you is assisting men who may have an aspiration for ministry leadership to taking on greater leadership roles in your church. Maybe they feel a sense of calling or at least a real aspiration to serve in ministry leadership and need a trusted place to grow. We want to help!

First of all, we want to encourage you to raise up men to be leaders in your church, here are a few questions.

Who do you identify as emerging leaders in your church?

Do you have a plan to help an emerging leader discern the call to ministry?

We do!

Let us help you mentor emerging leaders in your church who may have a sense of calling to the ministry. There are several good reasons for you to let us help you.

Provides a Place for Shared Growth

First, an Above Reproach group provides an opportunity for like-minded men to gather regularly and share their heart for ministry. Men are able to network with one another and share insights in a comfortable setting.

Opportunity to Learn from Varied Perspectives

Second, pastors within the association are encouraged to participate to share their testimonials and encourage these men. This provides an opportunity for pastors to see firsthand the Above Reproach concept and share their call-to-ministry stories with emerging leaders. It also provides an understanding of the broader scope of the reach of our church collectively within our association.

Provides a Formal Plan

Third, this process provides a platform where spiritual growth is encouraged through reading the written work of trusted authors to discuss in a controlled environment. It also provides an opportunity for men to learn how to develop expositional messages to other participants in a safe environment.

Next Steps

Above Reproach encourages men to take next steps. Those steps may be to lead a discipleship group, a small group, Sunday Bible class, participate in a mission trip, perhaps preach on a Sunday night, or engage in formal seminary training.

Why Encourage Participation within an Association of Churches?

Participate on an associational level is good for many reasons. First, it is a good place is to educate men about the true lack of the gospel message in our own backyards. There are thousands of people in every area in need of the gospel message. We have a network of churches that collaborating together can become stronger and work more effectively as a real force for good in our community to expand the church. It is noted that Paul had thirty-one coworkers sharing the gospel. Together we can do much more to broaden our footprint in our area and stretch and develop a mature kingdom mindset. Choosing to work on an association level strengthens the overall church in our area as we sow seeds and God provides the harvest.

The advantage of creating a group for your association is to cement the relationships between churches in your geographic area, both larger and smaller congregations

Appendix C

Mentoring Emerging Leaders Survey

In January 2024, while presenting a breakout session at the Midwest Leadership Summit held in Springfield, Illinois, 112 respondents completed a survey, and we would like to share the results. Even though this is a small sampling, from speaking with pastors at other conferences, this is indicative of the sentiment of ministry leaders. The biggest takeaway is that 62.5 percent of ministry leaders indicate there is no formalized process to mentor leaders in their church. The positive is that 90.2 percent of the respondents were willing to work with church leaders within their geographic region or association to mentor and disciple leaders. This is why we feel it is important for churches both larger and normative sized to cooperate together to mentor emerging leaders.

	Yes	No	N/A
Do you offer mentorship for men in your church?	59.8%	29.5%	1.8%
Are you actively mentoring leaders in your church?	72.3%	27.7%	
Do you have a formalized process they can participate at your local church or within your association of churches	37.5%	62.5%	
Do you have a culture within your church that makes men feel comfortable to explore the call to ministry?	72.3%	25.9%	1.8%
Would you be willing to cooperate with a process where (3-12 men meet) offered through your association or cooperating with other church leaders in your geographic area to mentor/disciple men as they explore next steps?	90.2%	8.0%	1.8%
Is creating a culture of developing men as leaders in your congregation important?	98.2%	0.9%	0.9%
Do you presently have men from your church taking seminary classes?	41.1%	58.9%	

N/A -Denotes No Response

Appendix D
Call to Ministry Book Resources

The Path to Being a Pastor by Bobby Jamieson

This book by Bobby Jamieson is excellent for a man with the aspiration to become involved in ministry leadership. In it, Jamieson explains why it's better to emphasize "aspiration" over "calling" as men pursue the office of elder and encourages readers to make sure they are pastorally gifted before considering the role. He shares from his own eleven-year experience preparing to be a pastor by walking potential leaders through different stages of ministry training, from practical steps—such as cultivating godly ambition and leadership, observing healthy churches, and mastering Scripture—to personal advice on building a strong family and succeeding in seminary. Emphasizing the importance of prayer, godly counsel, and immersion in the local church, Jamieson encourages men to ask *Am I qualified?* instead of *Am I called?* when considering a life in ministry.

Calling out the Called by Scott Pace and Shane Pruitt

This is a great book especially for a young man considering dedicating his life to ministry. Issues considered include wrestling with the call, abiding in Christ, loving the Scriptures, the importance of prayer, loving the church, relying on the Holy Spirit, serving others, balancing family life, persevering in ministry, and preparation. The book also begins with a charge to pastors to extend invitations, share testimonies, provide opportunities to engage individuals in ministry, and to be intentional about training emerging leaders.

Is God Calling Me? by Jeff Iorg

This book is written to a student and young adult audience, although it is applicable for all age groups. The author explores the foundational question that must be answered by anyone considering entry into ministry leadership: Is God calling me?

Discerning Your Call to Ministry: How to Know For Sure and What to Do about It by Jason K. Allen

In the preface, the author shares his personal journey of resisting God and the church as a young man until he gave his life to Christ in college. He then wrestled with a call to ministry. In this book he writes in a very intimate way, discussing the heavy topics of calling: Do you desire the ministry, character, having your personal house in order, your giftings, affirmation from your church, loving people, personal passion for the gospel and the Great Commission, what it means to be engaged in fruitful ministry, and to defend the faith. Finally, are you willing to truly surrender to God's call?

Am I Called? by Dave Harvey

Dave Harvey has been a pastor for over thirty years. In this book he is very straightforward about the requirements of following Christ. He divides the text into three sections: the first section addresses your calling to become a Christ follower, then your calling within the church. The second section provides the reader introspection of godly character, home life, preaching ability, shepherding the flock under your care, evangelism, and the call to ministry. The final portion is for all pastors to consider patience and the right attitude for service and sacrifice, realizing as God's workers we are always growing.

About Follow the Call

Our goal is to encourage pastors to invest in emerging leaders and raise up men to lead in every church!

> 98.2% of pastors believe creating a culture of developing men as leaders in their congregation is important.

Follow the Call Mission Statement

Follow the Call is dedicated to empowering men to follow God's call upon their heart to pursue ministry as pastors, preachers, and teachers of the Word and to mentor emerging leaders.

Calling out the called starts with ministry leaders, this is why we feel it is imperative for pastors to be intentional about raising men to be leaders in their church. We provide a platform to bolster the local pastor's ability to identify emerging leaders and provide resources to coach, mentor and care for these leaders. Our efforts involve a comprehensive approach to engaging local church leaders consisting of pastors, association leaders, and convention leaders to cooperate together. Our efforts are to bolster the church in the process of developing men wrestling with the call to ministry. We believe in the importance of fostering relationships in a regional context where churches help one another.

Above Reproach Groups

Our focus is upon **nurturing emerging leaders** within the local church community and feel this is accomplished through identifying, mentoring and caring for those who sense a call to ministry. A proven foundational tool to achieve this important mission is walking alongside a group of men and assisting them to take next steps as they discern the call to ministry. This is a proven methodology to invest in men, and what Tim LaFleur has coined as "an Above Reproach group."

An Above Reproach group consists of a pastor or ministry leader who walks alongside of three or more men wrestling with the call to ministry.

The group meets on a consistent basis for ten to twelve weeks, during which men are assigned a book to read about spiritual leadership or discipleship. Each week they discuss the assigned reading, talk about what is happening in their walk and everyday life, and pray for one another. As they walk through this process, they are also assigned a Scripture in one of Pastoral Epistles to develop an expositional sermon and present it to the group. This may seem a basic process; however, it provides a platform where men begin to discover if their calling is truly of God and something they should follow through upon or continue to discern.

We have found in some situations, a great way to formalize this process is on an associational level. This is where associational leaders are integral to encouraging pastors to invite men to be part of the Above Reproach process. This is especially helpful as multiple pastors become involved in the process, providing a greater variety of perspectives and insights to the mentees. An example would be for four pastors to be assigned to mentor and facilitate the group, with each pastor taking the lead for a three-week period. This is advantageous for several reasons. It provides structure for everyone involved, it fosters cooperation among pastors, and it creates a disciple-making culture for emerging leaders within an association. A key consideration for this approach is that many association leaders have a great depth of ministry experience. Their leadership provides pastors who encourage men to participate reassurance that those mentees participating will be provided a strong spiritual learning environment.

As part of our research, we asked pastors at a recent leadership conference to complete a survey, and the results provide strong evidence local church pastors would welcome this approach in their church association. Here are a couple of the questions and the response received.

"Would you be willing to cooperate with a process where (3–12 men meet) offered through your association with other church leaders in your geographic area to mentor/disciple men as they explore next steps?" 90.2 percent of the respondents said, "Yes!" This level of response provides strong evidence that many pastors are willing to cooperate with other church leaders within their geography to mentor emerging leaders. Once implemented, we believe the Above Reproach process will become an ongoing effort once or twice a year and provided continuity for leadership development and church growth within local associations.

We want to share one more statistic to emphasize the significance of leadership development within the church. We asked, "Is creating a culture of developing men as leaders in their congregation important?" 98.2% said, "Yes!" This is why we feel it is so essential to provide the Above Reproach group platform to the church as a means to walk alongside and develop emerging leaders. Not everyone is called to be a pastor, but many are called to lead in a variety of roles to carry out their God-given calling. It is through this process that some who may initially feel called to ministry and truly discern the call realize they are called to ministry, but not necessarily ministry leadership as a pastor or missionary.

Provide a Platform of Resources

One of our chief objectives is to be a resource for all things related to the call of ministry. In in an effort to achieve this aim, we have developed **FollowtheCall.org**. This online portal provides a list of reading resources related to the call to ministry, developing spiritual disciplines, discipleship and evangelism, leadership, preaching, church revitalization, and navigating mid-life decisions. We hope this resource will be helpful to assist pastor to provide a place for those navigating next steps to utilize as a knowledge hub.

Beyond reading resources are video testimonies from a variety of pastors and ministry leaders to aid those in the call process to identify with men who may have similar experiences to their own. It also provides an array of perspectives to gain a better grasp of steps involved in discernment. These testimonies are spoken in several languages including English, Spanish, Arabic, and Korean. We have also highlighted a variety of seminaries and learning institutions to make it easier for those who want to advance their education to explore options.

Programs

Follow the Call is developing a speaker's bureau of qualified men to preach at local churches, speak at association meetings and conferences to encourage leadership development and promote discipleship programs to encourage men who sense a call to ministry with next steps. We would love the opportunity to connect with those who aspire to be point men to assist in our cause, and also welcome the opportunity to connect with your local church or association.

We are available to speak at your local church or association conference on the topics of developing, equipping, and empowering emerging leaders with the church. Some of program topics and key points we emphasize include:

Developing Emerging Leaders

- Highlight the importance of identifying and nurturing potential leaders within the congregation.
- Share practical strategies for identifying leadership qualities in individuals.
- Discuss mentorship, training, and hands-on experience as essential components of leadership development.

Discipling Believers to Grow in Faith

- Emphasize the role of discipleship in spiritual growth.
- Encourage believers to engage in intentional relationships where they can be mentored and challenged.
- Discuss the significance of studying God's Word, prayer, and community in fostering faith maturity.

Coaching and Mentoring

- Explain the difference between coaching and mentoring.
- Provide examples of effective coaching and mentoring relationships.
- Encourage pastors and leaders to invest time in guiding and supporting others.

Caring for Emerging Leaders

- Address the challenges and pressures faced by emerging leaders.
- Discuss the importance of emotional and spiritual support.
- Encourage a culture of grace, accountability, and encouragement within the church.

Our prayer is that your passion for raising up leaders will inspire others to do the same. We hope that you will extend an invitation to our organization to deliver this message. We love to encourage and equip fellow pastors and believers to invest in the next generation of leaders!

A Final Word

We are all journeying together in this moment of time and have been graced by God to know Jesus as our Savior. There have been many disciples throughout the centuries who have discipled others and continued to pass the torch to lead the church. In this moment in our country, and in our world, it seems more than ever we need to double down on our effort to develop leaders and raise up men for the pastorate. <u>Every pastor</u> should train other men to be teachers in the church. *We have a very clear scriptural mandate.* The apostle Paul's instruction to Timothy applies to all pastors: "What you have heard from me in the presence of many witnesses entrust to faithful men who will be able to teach others also" (2 Timothy 2:2).

Will you help us to set ablaze many fires to raise up men to Follow the Call?

About the Authors

Rob and Tim have a heart to assist those in role of pastor both full-time and bi-vocationally to identify and mentor emerging leaders. They have a strong desire to aid the church to raise up a new generation of disciple makers, evangelists, pastors, and teachers of the Word.

Tim Lafleur

Tim LaFleur serves as the Director of Spiritual Formation for Follow the Call Ministries. Tim has served in a variety of ministry roles from the small to the megachurch environment. He served twenty years as the campus minister at Nicholls State University in Thibodaux, Louisiana. His two previous church assignments were at Brainerd Baptist Church in Chattanooga, Tennessee, and Long Hollow Baptist Church in Hendersonville, Tennessee. Presently, he is presently serving as the Equipping Pastor at Living Word Church in Houma, Louisiana. He received his undergraduate degree at Louisiana State University and Master's Degree. from Southwestern Baptist Theological Seminary.

Rob Millman

Rob Millman serves as the Executive Director of Follow the Call Ministries. Rob has served in many roles in the church, from Sunday School teacher and elder to a congregational lay leader. Professionally, he has taught high school agriculture and has worked in multiple roles as professional sales manager for both regional and national seed companies. He has been engaged in real estate brokerage for over twenty-five years. He presently operates a real estate brokerage in Indiana. Rob received his undergraduate degree from Purdue University and a Master's degree in Christian Ministry from Liberty University.

WHEN GOD CALLS SAY YES!

www.ingramcontent.com/pod-product-compliance
Lightning Source LLC
Chambersburg PA
CBHW070153100426
42743CB00013B/2900